Cambridge Elements ≡

Elements in the Problems of God
edited by
Michael L. Peterson
Asbury Theological Seminary

THE PROBLEM OF GOD IN DAVID HUME

Anders Kraal
The University of British Columbia Faculty of Arts

CAMBRIDGE
UNIVERSITY PRESS

Shaftesbury Road, Cambridge CB2 8EA, United Kingdom

One Liberty Plaza, 20th Floor, New York, NY 10006, USA

477 Williamstown Road, Port Melbourne, VIC 3207, Australia

314–321, 3rd Floor, Plot 3, Splendor Forum, Jasola District Centre, New Delhi – 110025, India

103 Penang Road, #05–06/07, Visioncrest Commercial, Singapore 238467

Cambridge University Press is part of Cambridge University Press & Assessment, a department of the University of Cambridge.

We share the University's mission to contribute to society through the pursuit of education, learning and research at the highest international levels of excellence.

www.cambridge.org
Information on this title: www.cambridge.org/9781009494465

DOI: 10.1017/9781009270243

First published 2023

A catalogue record for this publication is available from the British Library.

ISBN 978-1-009-49446-5 Hardback
ISBN 978-1-009-27026-7 Paperback
ISSN 2754-8724 (online)
ISSN 2754-8716 (print)

The Problem of God in David Hume

Elements in the Problems of God

DOI: 10.1017/9781009270243
First published online: December 2023

Anders Kraal
The University of British Columbia Faculty of Arts

Author for correspondence: Anders Kraal, anders.kraal@ubc.ca

Abstract: David Hume (1711–1776) is one of the foremost critics of attempts to provide rational arguments in support of traditional Christian theism in Western philosophy. In this Element, the author examines Hume's chief objections to the cosmological argument, the design argument, and the argument from miracles, along with some main responses to these objections. The author also examines Hume's seminal version of the argument from evil, which is deployed in an effort to show that traditional Christian theism is lacking in coherent meaning. Drawing on recent developments in Hume scholarship according to which Hume's ultimate philosophical aim was to further an anti-Christian agenda, an attempt is made to situate Hume's writings on God and religion in an unfolding narrative that is impacted throughout by the trenchant religious criticisms of Hume's chief philosophical predecessor, Thomas Hobbes.

Keywords: David Hume, cosmological arguments, design arguments, arguments from miracles, problem of evil

ISBNs: 9781009494465 (HB), 9781009270267 (PB), 9781009270243 (OC)
ISSNs: 2754-8724 (online), 2754-8716 (print)

Contents

1 Introduction   1

2 Overview of Hume's Life and Writings   2

3 The Starting Point: A Hobbesian Challenge to Traditional
   Christian Theism   10

4 Cosmological Arguments   16

5 Arguments from Design   24

6 Arguments from Miracles   31

7 Arguments from Evil   36

8 The End Result: A Turn to Hobbesian Theism   45

   References   51

1 Introduction

A 2014 survey of close to a thousand philosophy professors showed David Hume to be the most popular philosopher in English-language universities around the world (Bourget and Chalmers 2014, 476). Among the contributions for which Hume is often praised is his skepticism about the possibility of knowledge beyond experience, his rejection of the idea of a self, his attempts at a naturalistic account of morality without any appeal to normative facts, and, last but not least, his elaborate criticisms of the attempts of natural theology to provide rational support for belief in God. Hume's ideas on these various topics have significantly impacted the philosophical agenda down to the present day. Moreover, Hume's criticisms of natural theology have had a major impact on Western culture at large, having become part of "the mainstream of European thought" (Gaskin 2009, 509), and contributing in no small measure to the secularization of the Western mind.

There is good reason to think that the secularization of the Western mind was one of the intended aims of Hume's philosophizing. On his deathbed in 1776, Hume made an oft-cited admission to this effect to his friend Adam Smith. In Smith's public account of this admission, Hume imagined pleading with the mythological figure Charon for a little more time on Earth on the ground that he was "endeavoring to open the eyes of the public" and seeking "the downfall of some of the prevailing systems of superstition" (Kemp Smith 1947, 245). Moreover, Smith's private account identifies Hume's target not merely as "prevailing systems of superstition," but more specifically as "the churches" and "the clergy" (Mossner and Ross 1977, 204). This admission reveals an overtly anti-clerical, and perhaps even anti-Christian, aim on the part of Hume's philosophizing.

Hume's deathbed admission agrees with a recent turn in Hume scholarship, associated in particular with the work of Russell (2008, 2021), according to which the fundamental intention of Hume's philosophizing is "irreligion," or more specifically a Thomas Hobbes-inspired attempt to "discredit and refute Christian metaphysics and morals" (Russell 2008, x). This so-called Irreligious Interpretation of Hume contrasts with the two main earlier comprehensive interpretations of Hume in the literature, which identify Hume's fundamental intention with skepticism and naturalism respectively (see Fogelin 1985 and Kemp Smith 2005 for examples of the skeptical and naturalistic readings). The present study sympathizes with this recent "irreligious turn" in the literature.

Hume's irreligious project is pursued on a variety of different fronts, and in writings of a variety of different genres, including historical, moral, and metaphysical and epistemological. In the following, we focus on Hume's metaphysical and epistemological criticisms of traditional Christian theism, and in particular on two main themes running throughout these criticisms. The first theme is *that traditional Christian theism is lacking in rational demonstration*, and the second is the Hobbes-inspired claim *that traditional Christian theism lacks coherent meaning*. The first theme is pursued in Sections 4, 5, and 6, where we examine Hume's influential attempts to undermine traditional arguments for the existence of God. The second theme is introduced in Section 3, which presents Hobbes's challenge to the traditional Christian concept of God and Hume's initial response to it, and in Sections 7 and 8, where we examine at greater length how Hume deploys the problem of evil to launch an attack on the meaningfulness of traditional Christian theism which in turn lands him in the conclusion that the only philosophically viable form of theism is a form of Hobbesian theism.

That there are strong affinities between Hume's and Hobbes's thought on God is a central idea in Russell's Irreligious Interpretation (see, e.g., Russell 2008, 61–69). For Russell this affinity particularly concerns Hobbes's and Hume's empiricist accounts of meaning as applied to the idea of God. In what follows, I put the emphasis on an additional similarity, namely the view that the only form of theism that has a coherent meaning and at least some minimal rational support is something like the form of theism one finds in the work of Hobbes.

The aim of this study is not to provide a comprehensive survey of all major aspects of Hume's thought on God. Many excellent surveys of this sort already exist – J. C. A. Gaskin's *Hume's Philosophy of Religion* (1988), Keith Yandell's *Hume's "Inexplicable Mystery"* (1990), and Alan Bailey and Dan O'Brien's *Hume's Critique of Religion* (2014) being noteworthy examples. Rather, what this study aims to provide is an introductory text that situates Hume's thought on God within a unified and unfolding story. This story begins with the traditional Christian theism of Hume's youth; then moves on to consider Hume's thought on some of the great topics of eighteenth-century philosophy, such as the theistic arguments and the problem of evil, which were to occupy much of Hume's attention as an adult; and then concludes with what I propose is the end result of Hume's philosophical journey as regards the question of God, namely the belief that the only form of theism possessing a coherent meaning and at least some minimal rational support is something much like Hobbesian theism. However, in telling this story I will also seek to weave various philosophical responses to Hume's thought – both positive and negative, contemporaneous and more recent – into the overall narrative, so the study is at once both historical and philosophical.

2 Overview of Hume's Life and Writings

I start with an overview of Hume's life and writings. Hume's thought on God and religion developed in the very specific cultural circumstances of early eighteenth-century Scotland. To better understand the development of his thought, we do well to gather a general picture of these cultural circumstances, and how they relate to his writings.

2.1 Religion in Early Eighteenth-Century Scotland

Hume was born in Edinburgh in 1711, and grew up in Ninewells some forty miles south-east of Edinburgh. He was baptized as an infant into the Church of Scotland, or "Kirk," and was raised a Presbyterian Christian. His family attended the weekly Sunday services at the local Chirnside Parish Church, where his uncle, George Home, was minister.

The Kirk had been the official church of Scotland since the Revolution of 1688–1689, with the *Westminster Confession* as its official creed (Burleigh 1960, 261–263). This creed affirms well-known Christian doctrines, such as God as triune; the fall of man into sin; the incarnation of the Son of God in Jesus Christ; and so on. But in addition to these generic Christian doctrines, a further set of doctrines not shared widely by other Christian churches were also affirmed, in particular the predestinarian doctrine that God has foreordained some humans to everlasting salvation and others to everlasting damnation "according to the unsearchable counsel of his own will, whereby he extendeth or withholdeth mercy as he pleaseth" (Leith 1973, 199). As this doctrine traces back to the Protestant theologian John Calvin (1509–1564), the Scottish Presbyterian theology of the *Westminster Confession* is often characterized as "Calvinistic."

During the first few decades of the eighteenth century, the Kirk took Scottish society in the direction of a tightened confessionalization. Ministers were required to declare adherence to the *Westminster Confession*, and measures were introduced to bring the four Scottish universities – Edinburgh, Glasgow, St. Andrews, and Aberdeen – into alignment with Calvinist theology. Anglican-leaning faculty were replaced by professors adhering to the *Westminster Confession*, and as a result the Scottish university system came to "reflect the values of the presbyterian burghers who governed it and the presbyterian churchmen who served as its administrators and supervised its curriculum with careful scrutiny" (Sher 1990, 9).

In Scottish society at large, regular church attendance was the norm, and the Calvinist theology of the *Westminster Confession* provided the doctrinal content also of the popular sermons of the day (Graham 1901, 400). Devotional literature was the most widely read type of literature throughout the whole eighteenth century. The writings of Thomas Boston (1676–1732), the most famous preacher of his generation, went through 150 editions, more than any other writings (Ryken 1995, 298). A vivid picture of the theology permeating Hume's youth is provided by Boston's *Human Nature in Its Fourfold State* (1720), the single most widely reprinted book in eighteenth-century Scotland, and a well-known book also in Hume's household (Mossner 1980, 285). Boston discourses on four "states" of human nature: the "state of innocence" in which humans were originally created; the "state of nature" that followed upon their fall into sin; the "state of grace" following upon regeneration by the Holy Spirit; and the "eternal state" of either blessedness in heaven or torment in hell. Boston's depiction of eternal torment is graphic and chilling:

> But they shall be miserable beyond expression, in a relative separation from God. Though he will be present in the very centre of their souls, if I may so express it, while they are wrapped up in fiery flames, in utter darkness; it shall only be to feed them with the vinegar of his wrath, and to punish them with the emanations of his revenging justice: they shall never more taste of his goodness and bounty, nor have the least glimpse of hope from him. (Boston 1841, 345)

Boston's book culminates in a call to accept God's offer of salvation:

> The avenger of blood is pursuing thee, O sinner; haste and escape to the city of refuge. Wash now in the fountain of the Mediator's blood, that you may not perish in the lake of fire. Open thy heart to him, lest the pit close its mouth on thee. Leave thy sins, else they will ruin thee: kill them, else they will be thy death for ever. (Boston 1841, 357)

These were the sorts of calls to repentance and faith that the young Hume would have grown up listening to.

2.2 Religious Upbringing and Crisis

Hume appears to have taken a deep interest in the topic of God at least since his early youth. His earliest reading notes, the so-called Memoranda from his teens or 20s (the exact dating is a matter of dispute), are often concerned with God. Examples of things he jotted down include the following remarks:

> Three kinds of Atheists according to some. 1. Who deny the Existence of a God. Such as Diagoras, Theodorus. 2. Who deny a Providence, Such as the Epicureans & the Ionic Sect. 3. Who deny the Freewill of the Deity, Such as Aristotle, the Stoics. &c . . .
>
> God cou'd have prevented all Abuses of Liberty without taking away Liberty. Therefore Liberty no Solution of Difficultys . . .
>
> Three Proofs for the Existence of a God. 1. something necessarily existent, & what is so is infinitely perfect. 2. The Idea of Infinite must come from an infinite Being. 3. The Idea of infinite Perfection implys that of actual Existence. (Mossner 1948, 501–502)

Hume was religiously devout in his youth. In a report of his deathbed interview with Hume in 1776, James Boswell recalls that he asked Hume

> if he was not religious when he was young. He said he was, and he used to read *The Whole Duty of Man*; that he made an abstract from the Catalogue of vices at the end of it, and examined himself by this ... (Scott and Pottle 1931, 227)

However, at some point during his adolescence – we don't know exactly when – Hume had a religious crisis. Our principal source for this is a 1751 letter from Hume to a friend. Discussing the manuscript of what was to become the *Dialogues concerning Natural Religion*, he says that

> tis not long ago that I burn'd an old Manuscript Book, wrote before I was twenty; which contain'd, Page after Page, the gradual Progress of my Thoughts on that head. It began with an anxious Search after Arguments, to confirm the common Opinion: Doubts stole in, dissipated, return'd, were again dissipated, return'd again; and it was a perpetual Struggle of a restless Imagination against Inclination, perhaps against Reason. (Greig 1932, 154)

Since this crisis is related to the contents of the *Dialogues concerning Natural Religion*, it appears that it was induced by a study of arguments for and against the existence of God, since this is the content of that book.

In Boswell's aforementioned interview, Hume said that "he never entertained any belief in Religion since he began to read Locke and Clarke" (Scott and Pottle 1931, 76). It is not entirely clear from this remark exactly what role Locke and Clarke played in his religious crisis, although it is clear that they played some role. Locke and Clarke had both argued for the existence of God on the basis of different versions of the cosmological argument (see, e.g., Locke 1706, 529–530 and Clarke 1705). Hume also displays an awareness of this in the *Dialogues concerning Natural Religion*, describing Locke as "the first Christian" to base "the principles of theology" on "a chain of arguments," and then going on to single out Clarke's cosmological argument as a principal target (Hume 1779, 35, 165). This suggests that Hume's crisis might have been induced by worries over what was perceived as Locke's and Clarke's failure to establish the existence of God by means of rational arguments.

At some point, after his loss of faith, when he was roughly in his mid-twenties, Hume set about working on his first major writing project, *A Treatise of Human Nature*. This was the first of many literary projects spanning a time frame of roughly forty years, leading all the way up to his death at age 65, with a few works appearing posthumously as well. The topic of God is a recurring theme in these writings. Indeed, Hume scholar James Noxon has estimated that "Hume spent more of his pages on the topic of religion than on any other" (Noxon 1976, 59). In what follows,

I outline the circumstances of Hume's more important works bearing on religious themes, situating them in the broader context of Hume's life.

2.3 Hume's Literary Career

A Treatise of Human Nature (henceforth *Treatise*) was published in 1739–1740, when Hume was around 29. Most of what we know about its prehistory can be gleaned from some brief remarks in Hume's correspondence as well as from a few autobiographical lines in "My Own Life." In one of his earliest preserved letters, dated 1734, Hume remarks that "a new Scene of Thought" opened up to him at age 18 (Greig 1932, 13–14). In another letter, from 1751, he says that the *Treatise* was "plan'd before I was one and twenty, & compos'd before twenty five" (Greig 1932, 158). In "My Own Life" he says that the *Treatise* was written "[d]uring my retreat in France" (Kemp Smith 1947, 234). Piecing these remarks together, Ernest Mossner suggests that the *Treatise* was composed in three phases: planned in 1726–1729, drafted in 1729–1733, and completed in 1733–1736 during a two-year retreat in France (Mossner 1980, 74).

Around the time of the completion of the *Treatise*, Hume started reaching out to public intellectuals in both England and Scotland. He contacted Joseph Butler, a Bishop of the Church of England widely known for his work in Christian apologetics, on account of whom Hume admitted to having toned down parts of the *Treatise* (dealing with miracles) so as not to offend (see Greig 1932, 25.) Hume also contacted Francis Hutcheson, Scotland's best-known philosophy professor at the time, and leader of a moderated Presbyterianism that had begun to make inroads in Scotland in the 1730s (Greig 1932, 32–40).

There is considerable disagreement in the literature as regards the ultimate aim of Hume's *Treatise*, and how it relates to religion. Since there is little explicit mention of religious themes in the book, many have concluded that the book was not intended to contribute to the lively debates about God going on at that time, but was instead more concerned with developing the consequences of skepticism or naturalism (see, e.g., Mossner 1980, 113; Flew 1961, 11; Gaskin 1988, 1–2). In more recent years, Paul Russell has argued that this is a mistake, and that "problems of religion, broadly conceived … hold the contents of the *Treatise* together as a unified work" (Russell 2008, x).

Hume's second major work, originally entitled *Philosophical Essays concerning Human Understanding*, and later renamed *An Enquiry concerning Human Understanding* (henceforth *Enquiry*), from 1748, was published almost a decade after the *Treatise*. In "My Own Life" Hume describes this book as the outcome of an attempt to convert the theoretical parts of the *Treatise* into a more appealing and accessible form:

> I had always entertained a notion, that my want of success in publishing the *Treatise of Human Nature*, had proceeded more from the manner than the matter [. . .] I, therefore, cast the first part of that work anew in the Enquiry concerning Human Understanding . . . (Kemp Smith 1947, 235)

Recent scholarship suggests that there may have been more going on. According to M. A. Stewart, one factor that likely played an important role in Hume's writing of this book was his failure in 1744 to obtain a professorial chair in philosophy at Edinburgh University. Hume's candidacy was defeated by the veto of the Presbyterian clergy, which had sensed irreligion in Hume's *Treatise*. In his private correspondence, Hume complained about having been defeated by "the bigotry of the clergy" (Greig 1932, 62). According to Stewart, the *Enquiry* was part of "an aggressive polemic against attitudes of the kind that had blocked his appointment" (Stewart 1995, 22). Evidence for this suggestion is found in the work itself, which argues strongly against theistic arguments, the credibility of miracle reports, and the moral and social value of religion. Further evidence is found in Hume's private correspondence; in a letter from 1747, Hume justifies going ahead with the publication of the book on the ground that he is "too deep engaged to think of a retreat," having now been outed as "an infidel" (Greig 1932, 106). Stewart's suggestion has gained traction in the literature (see, e.g., Beauchamp 2000, xvii).

Shortly after the *Enquiry*, Hume started working on the *Enquiry concerning the Principles of Morals*, published 1751, which was an attempt to cast the ethical parts of the *Treatise* into a more accessible form. Pretty much all we know about the circumstances of its composition are found in this passage of Hume's "My Own Life":

> I went down in 1749 and lived two Years with my Brother at his Country house: For my Mother was now dead. I there composed . . . my Enquiry concerning the Principles of Morals, which is another part of my Treatise, that I cast anew. (Kemp Smith 1947, 235)

Although this book doesn't contain any explicit discussion of religious topics, there are occasional derogatory remarks on Christian morality. For example, Hume brands humility a vice rather than a virtue, in explicit contrast to what he calls "monkish virtues" (Hume 1751, 174). This was a transvaluation of the religious morality of Hume's Presbyterian upbringing. Due to remarks like this, the book has been described as "a clear rejection of Christian ethics" (Beauchamp 2009, 49).

Hume's next major book project was the *History of England*, published in six volumes throughout 1754–1762. First out were two volumes on the Stuarts, in 1754 and 1757, followed by two volumes on the Tudors in 1759, followed by two concluding volumes in 1762 on the period from the invasion of Julius Caesar to Henry VII.

In "My Own Life," Hume says that this history project was sparked by his appointment as librarian in Edinburgh in 1752, giving him "command of a large library" (Kemp Smith 1947, 236). On a philosophical level, scholars have described this project as motivated in part by Hume's religious criticism (see, e.g., Foster 1997, 1–24). For example, in the first volume from 1754, Hume characterized the two driving forces of Stuart history as Protestant "enthusiasm" and Catholic "superstition," two forces which he believed had caused England countless woes. Also, when Hume got around to describing the Reformation in Scotland in the two 1759 volumes, the Protestant reformer and national hero John Knox is portrayed as a bigoted fanatic. This portrayal provoked a negative backlash in Scotland, and in a letter to Adam Smith from 1759, Hume reports that "all the Godly in Scotland abuse me for my Account of John Knox & the Reformation" (Klibansky and Mossner 1954, 55).

It was partly on account of the history volumes that there was a highly publicized and concerted effort in 1755 to formally excommunicate Hume from the Kirk (Mossner 1980, 338–355). An accusation had been brought before the Kirk's ruling body, the General Assembly, according to which Hume had, among other things, characterized the Reformation as "the work of madmen" (Mossner 1980, 342). In response, the General Assembly adopted a resolution condemning this characterization, but stopping short of a formal excommunication. This leniency is often ascribed to the emergence of a new "Moderate Party" in the Kirk at this time, led by the influential Edinburgh clergymen William Robertson, Principal of Edinburgh University, who was on friendly terms with Hume. Although not explicitly opposed to the Calvinist theology of the Westminster Confession, the Moderate Party lacked the dogmatic zeal of the more traditional Calvinists (for more, see Sher 1985 and Burleigh 1960, 286–308).

In 1756, a year after the Kirk's official censure, and parallel with his work on the *History of England*, Hume planned to publish a highly controversial collection of essays to be entitled "Five Dissertations." This collection was to include the three highly controversial essays "The Natural History of Religion," "Of Suicide," and "Of the Immortality of the Soul" (for a detailed account, see Mossner 1980, 319–335). Hume's publisher Andrew Millar had the collection printed and circulated some copies prior to the official publication date. One of these copies ended up in the hands of William Warburton, a Bishop of the Church of England, who found the contents subversive to the point of meriting legal prosecution, for which purpose he enlisted some prominent British lawyers. Upon hearing this, Millar cancelled the scheduled publication.

A toned-down version of "The Natural History of Religion" appeared in the collection *Four Dissertations* from the following year, 1757. The essays "Of

Suicide" and "Of the Immortality of the Soul" were not published until 1777, however, a year after Hume's death, when they came out under the title *Two Essays*. "The Natural History of Religion," which is much longer than the other essays in the original collection, is today often published as a free-standing book. Hume's contemptuous reference in "My Own Life" to "the illiberal petulance, arrogance, and scurrility" of "the Warburtonian school" is to be seen against the background of this episode (Kemp Smith 1947, 237).

Hume's last book, the *Dialogues concerning Natural Religion* (henceforth *Dialogues*), is mentioned for the first time in a letter from 1751, that is, from around the period of the two Enquiries (Greig 1932, 154). It is brought up again in a letter from 1763, in which Hume responds to a Presbyterian clergyman's advice to either suppress the book or at least postpone its publication (Klibansky and Mossner 1954, 72–73). After this, we do not hear much about the book until 1776, the year of Hume's death, when Hume polished the manuscript further and requested his friends William Strahan and Adam Smith to take care of its publication after his passing (Klibansky and Mossner 1954, 322–324). As they were both reluctant to meet this request, the publication of the book was ultimately ensured by Hume's nephew, David Hume the Younger, in 1779, two years after Hume's death (Klibansky and Mossner 1954, 453–454). Although the *Dialogues* is today widely recognized as one of the most important books of all times in the philosophy of religion, the book did not cause much of a stir when first published, contrary to the expectations of Strahan and Smith.

As an expression of Hume's own views on God, the *Dialogues* is an unusually difficult work to interpret. The book presents a dialogue between three main characters, Cleanthes, Demea, and Philo, but it is not said which of these, if any, represents Hume. Cleanthes is said to represent "the accurate philosophical turn"; Demea "rigid inflexible orthodoxy"; and Philo "careless scepticism" (Hume 1779, 10). Most commentators take Philo to speak for Hume (see, e.g., Kemp Smith 1947, 73–96). And there are good reasons for this; for example, Hume has Philo "come out in the open as victor" in Dialogue X (Kemp Smith 1947, 87). But Philo is also represented in ways that it is unlikely Hume would have identified with; for example, Philo comes down as a friend of Christianity in Dialogue XII, saying that being "a philosophical Sceptic" is "a first and most essential step towards being a sound, believing Christian" (Hume 1779, 154). Perhaps the most defensible view would be to regard Philo as oftentimes representative of Hume's thought, but not always. This approach has been urged by commentators such as Hendel (1963, 271) and Jeffner (1966, 208), and will also be the favored approach in the present study.

3 The Starting Point: A Hobbesian Challenge to Traditional Christian Theism

The Presbyterian church of Hume's upbringing took God to be a being with attributes such as infinite power, knowledge, and goodness. This theological doctrine of God was not unique to the Calvinist theology of the *Westminster Confession*, but was shared also by other traditional Christian churches, such as the Anglican church, the Lutheran churches, and the Roman Catholic church (see, e.g., the creeds of these churches in Leith 1973). In what follows, I shall refer to this doctrine of God as "the traditional Christian doctrine of God," or "traditional Christian theism."

The traditional Christian doctrine of God corresponds to what in seventeenth- and eighteenth-century philosophy was often termed "the idea of God": the idea of a being who is infinitely powerful, knowledgeable, good, and so on. Traditional Christian theism provided the doctrinal backdrop for the typical list of divine attributes taken to make up the idea of God in philosophy, although it is worth keeping in mind that the traditional Christian doctrine of God was typically taken to comprise doctrines that were taken to lie beyond the field of philosophy proper, such as that God is triune, or that the Son of God became incarnate in Jesus Christ. These latter doctrines do not typically enter into seventeenth- and eighteenth-century philosophical discussions of the idea of God.

The extent to which the *idea* of God was believed to adequately represent the *nature* of God was a question that had been discussed by theologians and philosophers long before the beginning of seventeenth- or eighteenth-century philosophy. But the question received a new impetus in the early modern period on account of the work of Thomas Hobbes (1588–1679), to whose work we must accordingly briefly turn. (My outline of Hobbes's challenge to traditional Christian theism and of the main responses to it in seventeenth- and eighteenth-century philosophy is much indebted to Russell 2008, 86–92.)

3.1 Hobbes's Challenge

In his exchange with Descartes, published in Descartes's *Objections and Replies* (1641), and later also in his *Leviathan* (1651), Hobbes claimed that humans can form no idea of God. The reasoning for this claim is put forth as follows in the *Leviathan*:

> Whatsoever we imagine is *finite*. Therefore there is no idea, or conception of any thing we call *infinite*. No man can have in his mind an image of infinite magnitude; nor conceive infinite swiftness, infinite time, or infinite force, or infinite power ... And therefore the name of God is used, not to make us conceive him; (for he is incomprehensible; and his greatness and power are

inconceivable;) but that we may honour him. Also because whatsoever . . . we conceive, has been perceived first by sense, either all at once, or by parts; a man can have no thought, representing any thing, not subject to sense. (Hobbes 1998, 19)

Hobbes's rejection of the idea of God is notoriously elusive. Is he saying only that humans cannot form a pictorial representation of God in their minds, or is he saying that humans cannot conceive of God at all? There is reason to think that he might in fact be saying the latter, for he explicitly contrasts his position with Descartes, and Descartes certainly did not think it possible for humans to form a pictorial representation of God, as he makes clear in many places (see, e.g., Descartes 1984, 127).

As is clear from the above quotation, Hobbes bases his rejection of the idea of God on two main considerations. First, he holds that humans are capable of forming ideas only of finite things. Since what is said to be the idea of God purports to be an idea of something infinite, it follows that humans cannot form any such idea. Second, he holds that humans are capable of forming ideas only of sensory objects. Since what is said to be the idea of God purports to be an idea of something that is not empirical, it follows, once again, that humans cannot form any such idea.

Despite rejecting the idea of God, Hobbes held that philosophical reasoning along lines of a basic version of the cosmological argument can validly lead humans to the belief that there is an eternal cause of the world. Says Hobbes:

Curiosity, or love of the knowledge of causes, draws a man from the consideration of the effect, to seek the cause; and again, the cause of that cause; till of necessity he must come to this thought at last, that there is some cause, whereof there is no former cause, but is eternal; though they cannot have any idea of him in their mind, answerable to his nature. (Hobbes 1998, 70)

Hobbes also maintains that one can acknowledge this eternal cause with honorific ascriptions such as "powerful," "good," "knowledgeable," and so on, even though these terms do not correspond to anything real in God's nature:

men that by their own meditation, arrive to the acknowledgement of one infinite, omnipotent, and eternal God, chose rather to confess he is incomprehensible, and above their understanding, than to define his nature by *spirit incorporeal*, and then confess their definition to be unintelligible: or if they give him such a title, it is not *dogmatically*, with intention to make the divine nature understood; but piously, to honour him with attributes, of significations, as remote as they can from the grossness of bodies visible. (Hobbes 1998, 73)

The possibility of acknowledging an eternal cause of the world while simultaneously being unable to form an idea of this cause was illustrated by the simile of a blind man standing before a fire who despite being unable to form an idea of the shape or color of fire can still feel its effects, and so can recognize that there is something that makes him hot (Hobbes 1998, 78–79). (For more on Hobbes's minimalistic theism, see Condren 2000, 54–59 and Martinich 2005, 200–207.)

Hobbes's rejection of the idea of God set the stage for a lively debate in seventeenth- and eighteenth-century philosophy. Hobbes's approach was challenged by a number of alternatives which were to form the background and context for Hume's own thinking about the idea of God. The approaches that were particularly important were the rationalistic approaches of Descartes and Samuel Clarke, the empiricist approach of Locke, and the analogical approach of William King. In what follows, I briefly outline these approaches before turning to Hume's own position on this topic (for more detail, see Russell 2008, 86–92).

3.2 Descartes's and Clarke's Rationalistic Responses

Descartes's rationalistic approach involves an appeal to innate ideas. Taking as his starting-point that we find an idea of God within ourselves, Descartes asks where this idea comes from. Reflection on this idea leads Descartes to conclude that the idea could not be produced by ourselves, since we are finite whereas the content of this idea is that of a complete or actual infinity, which nothing finite could possibly produce. This leads Descartes to conclude that the idea of God is not derived from our senses but is instead implanted in us (see, e.g., Descartes 1985, 305).

Clarke's approach is not rationalistic in the sense of Descartes's, as it steers clear of an appeal to innate ideas, but it is still rationalistic in that it holds that humans are capable of rationally intuiting certain fundamental principles – such as that whatever begins to exist must have a cause – which can then be used to infer that there must exist a cause corresponding to our idea of God (Clarke 1705, 75). The idea of God can accordingly be arrived at by means of a demonstration based on rationally intuited fundamental principles.

3.3 Locke's Empiricist Response

Locke's empiricist approach agrees with Hobbes that all of our ideas are derived empirically through our senses, but contends, against Hobbes, that it is perfectly possible to derive also the idea of God in this way. The idea of God, he says, is obtained by fusing the empirically derived ideas of "infinity," "existence," "power," "knowledge," and "goodness" together, hereby yielding the complex idea of an infinitely powerful, knowing and good existence (Locke 1706, 267).

The ideas of existence, power, knowledge, and goodness are held to derive from our experience, for we experience ourselves as existing, and we know from experience what it means to have some degree of power, knowledge, and goodness.

The idea of "infinity" is a bit harder to explain empirically. Locke rejects Descartes's view that we have an idea of an actual or complete infinity, proposing instead that we start from the experience of "any bulk of Matter," and then imagine this matter being divided into smaller and smaller parts indefinitely, which, he suggests, gives us an idea of infinity (Locke 1706, 173). By then fusing the idea of infinity with the ideas of existence, power, knowledge, and goodness, we are able to augment the latter ideas into the complex idea of an infinitely powerful, knowing, and good existence, that is, into the idea of God.

3.4 King's Analogical Response

King's analogical approach was widely influential in Hume's day, especially among more traditional, religious writers (see Berman 1983). King grants that the human mind has direct access only to sensory objects, and forms its ideas on this basis. But this is not taken to preclude the possibility of applying these ideas analogously to what is taken to lie beyond the empirical realm, on the basis of a presumed resemblance or likeness, and this is in fact what humans do in the case of the idea of God. For example, believing that the world we experience exhibits an order and arrangement which we cannot imagine being produced without great knowledge and power, our minds are led to suppose that the cause of the world must likewise possess attributes resembling what we call knowledge and power, and so we apply the ideas of knowledge and power to this eternal cause by way of analogy. Since the eternal cause to which the ideas of knowledge and power are analogously applied is not taken to be anything human, the nature of the attributes picked out by the analogously applied ideas are deemed "altogether different" from the nature of the attributes picked out by these ideas when applied to humans (King 1709, 5–6).

3.5 Hume's Initial Lockean Sympathies

Let us now turn to Hume. Hume's first book, the *Treatise*, contains no extensive discussion of Hobbes's rejection of the idea of God, nor of any of the alternative approaches outlined earlier. However, the book does contain implicit rejections of Descartes's and Clarke's rationalist approaches to the idea of God, as well as a few claims that place him, at least initially, in the Lockean camp.

Against Descartes's approach, Hume reiterates the basic empiricist theory of ideas of Hobbes and Locke, a consequence of which is a rejection of any innate ideas, including any innate idea of God (see *Treatise* 1.1.1). All ideas are said to be either complex or simple; if they are complex they are made up of simples; if they are simple they derive from "impressions," that is, sensations, feelings, emotions, and passions, or, in a word, from experience. The claim that all ideas derive from impressions is taken to be evident on the basis of an introspective review of our ideas: in conducting such a review we never come across a complex idea that is not reducible to simple ideas, and we never come across a simple idea that does not correspond to an impression. Since an innate idea would be an idea for which there is no corresponding impression, it follows that it is equally evident that there are no innate ideas, and hence, by implication, no innate idea of God.

Against Clarke's rationalist approach, we find Hume using his empiricist theory of ideas to impugn the supposedly intuitive principle that every effect must have a cause. This principle asserts a "necessary connection" between cause and effect, but Hume contends that the idea of any such connection lacks a corresponding impression, since all that is actually experienced is a constant conjunction between one event and another, and so the idea of a necessary connection is an idea in name only. Since Clarke's rationalist account of the idea of God is an attempt to infer this idea from a supposed necessary connection between cause and effect, it fails (see *Treatise* 1.1.1.6–7).

So Hume is clearly opposed to Descartes's and Clarke's rationalist approaches to the idea of God. As regards his view of the approaches of Hobbes, Locke, and King, things are more difficult, for it appears that he favors Locke in the *Treatise*, *Enquiry*, and *The Natural History of Religion*, but then shifts to favoring Hobbes in the *Dialogues*.

That Hume does not initially favor a Hobbesian approach is supported by passages where he recognizes that humans do indeed have an idea of God. For example, in *Treatise* 1.3.7.4 he says that "[to] think of God" involves having "[an] idea of him" (Hume 1739, 169), and later on, in *Treatise* 1.3.14.10, he says that "if every idea be deriv'd from an impression, the idea of a deity proceeds from the same origin" (Hume 1739, 281). These passages clearly imply that humans do have an idea of God, contrary to Hobbes's contention. Moreover, in the "Abstract," written in defense of the *Treatise*, we find Hume even more clearly favoring a Lockean account, for he says there that "our idea of a Deity" is "a composition of those ideas, which we acquire from reflecting on the operations of our own minds" (Hume 1740, 23). Moreover, since Hume makes no mention here of the relevant ideas being applied in an analogous sense to God, it appears that he favors a Lockean account also over against King's analogical alternative.

In Hume's *Enquiry* an unmistakably Lockean account of the origination of the idea of God is once again presented. After having reiterated the same empiricist theory of the origin of ideas that is found in the *Treatise*, he goes on to apply this theory explicitly to the idea of God:

> The idea of God, as meaning *an infinitely intelligent, wise, and good Being,*
> arises from reflecting on the operations of our own mind, and augmenting,
> without limit, those qualities of goodness and wisdom. (Hume 1748, 24–25)

This is about as succinct a statement on the derivation of the idea of God that can
be found in Hume. On the basis chiefly of this passage, many Hume scholars
ascribe a Lockean rather than a Hobbesian account of the idea of God to Hume
(see, e.g., Gaskin 1988, 99; Bailey and O'Brien 2014, 71).

In *The Natural History of Religion*, we find what is in effect an attempt to
anchor a Lockean account of the origination of the idea of God in a process of
cultural evolution. The idea of God, specified as the idea of an "omniscient,
omnipotent, and omnipresent" being, is said to have developed piecemeal out of
a prior and more anthropomorphic idea of "a powerful, though limited being, with
human passions and appetites, limbs and organs" (Hume 1757, 5). Hume characterizes the emergence of the former idea out of the latter as a "natural process":

> It seems certain, that, according to the natural process of human thought, the
> ignorant multitude must first entertain some groveling and familiar notion of
> superior powers, before they stretch their conception of that perfect Being,
> who bestowed order on the whole frame of nature. (Hume 1757, 5)

One of the chief aims of Hume's *The Natural History of Religion* is to explain
how the idea of God developed out of the idea of this anthropomorphic deity, and
also how the idea of this anthropomorphic deity developed in the first place. The
basic contention is that belief in invisible, intelligent power is a natural outcome
of the human condition (Hume 1757, 5). Hume characterizes the human condition, especially in earlier phases of human society, as a "disordered scene" (Hume
1757, 15). In this disordered scene human life is dominated by such things as
"appetite for food," "dread of future misery," "anxious concern for happiness,"
and "thirst for revenge," and humans find themselves in a "perpetual suspense
between life and death" (Hume 1757, 16–18). Not understanding the true causes
of fortune and misfortune, the human imagination is "employed in forming ideas
of those powers on which we have so entire a dependence" (Hume 1757, 16).
Seeking to form ideas of these powers, our mind

> rises gradually, from inferior to superior: by abstracting from what is imper-
> fect, it forms an idea of perfection: and slowly distinguishing the nobler parts
> of its own frame from the grosser, it learns to transfer only the former, much
> elevated and refined, to its divinity. (Hume 1757, 5)

By experience, we find that we possess various properties, and we single out
those properties that we find most admirable and then "transfer" them to the
power we believe is the cause of our fortune or misfortune, the outcome of

which is the idea of an anthropomorphic deity. When we transfer also our "passions and infirmities to the deity," the result is a deity who is "jealous and revengeful, capricious and partial, and, in short, a wicked and foolish man" (Hume 1757, 18).

Once the idea of this anthropomorphic divinity was up and running, the stage was set for the development of the full-blown idea of God, for humans were keen on seeking to gain favor with this divinity:

> supposing him to be pleased, like themselves, with praise and flattery, there is no eulogy or exaggeration which will be spared in their addresses to him [. . .] and even he who outdoes his predecessors in swelling up the titles of his divinity, is sure to be outdone by his successors in newer and more pompous epithets of praise. Thus they proceed; till at last they arrive at infinity itself, beyond which there is no farther progress. (Hume 1757, 46)

In this way, the human mind is taken to have arrived at the idea of God understood as an omniscient, omnipotent, and omnipresent being.

Interestingly, in his last main treatment of the idea of God, in the *Dialogues*, the thrust of Hume's philosophizing shifts markedly from a Lockean approach toward a more Hobbesian approach, as we will have occasion to see in Sections 7 and 8. But in his earlier work, as we have seen in this section, he exhibits clear Lockean sympathies, at least if taken at face value.

4 Cosmological Arguments

Assuming, at least provisionally, that the idea of God makes sense, Hume proceeds to offer highly influential criticisms of two major types of argument for the existence of God, the cosmological argument (or "argument a priori" in Hume's vocabulary) and the design argument (or "argument a posteriori"). We start with the cosmological argument, and turn to the design argument in the next section.

It is today widely recognized that there is strictly speaking no such thing as *the* cosmological argument, but rather a whole family of structurally similar versions of a type of argument that we for convenience can call the cosmological argument. Hume discusses and criticizes one specific version of this argument in various places in his works. The version that he appears to have had in mind is Samuel Clarke's argument as developed in *A Demonstration of the Being and Attributes of God* (1705). This is indicated by at least three things. First, in discussing the argument in the *Dialogues*, Hume refers to Clarke by name, even quoting from the *Demonstration* (Hume 1779, 165). Second, in stating the argument in the *Dialogues*, Hume makes use of terms that closely parallel Clarke's terms in the *Demonstration* (for details, see Stewart 1985, 247). And third, in responding to criticisms that his theory of causation undermines theistic arguments, Hume explicitly concedes that it does indeed undermine "Dr. Clark's Argument" (Hume 1967, 23). In seeking to understand Hume's criticisms of the cosmological argument, we accordingly do well to first gather a general understanding of Clarke's version of the argument.

4.1 The Targeted Argument in Outline

Clarke's version of the cosmological argument remains to this day a respected argument in philosophy, and has been deemed one of the best versions of the argument by prominent theists and nontheists alike, including Swinburne (1991, 119) on the theist side and Rowe (1975, 56) on the nontheist side.

Clarke's argument is presented as a sequence of twelve propositions each of which is provided with one or more separate demonstrations. Paraphrasing somewhat, the first three propositions assert that

(1) there exists something eternal;
(2) that this thing is not dependent on anything for its existence; and
(3) that this thing is necessarily existing. (Clarke 1705, 18, 24, 27)

These propositions form what is sometimes called "the first part" of the argument, meaning its foundation (see Rowe 1975, 57). The remaining nine propositions, or "second part" of the argument, take (1)–(3) as given and go on to affirm that

(4) we can form no positive idea of the essence of this being;
(5) that we nevertheless know that it has various essential attributes;
(6) that these attributes include its existing everywhere and always; as well as its
(7) oneness;
(8) intelligence;
(9) liberty and choice;
(10) power;
(11) wisdom; and
(12) goodness, justice, and truth (Clarke 1705, 81–233).

Each of these propositions is provided with a supplementary line of reasoning aimed at making it evident. As Hume's criticisms of the argument focus on propositions (1), (3), and (8) (as we shall see shortly), it is fitting to take a closer look at Clarke's reasoning specifically for these claims.

Proposition (1), then, says that there exists something eternal, something that has always existed. The supplementary reasoning for this claim goes as follows:

> Since something now is, it is evident that something always was, otherwise the things that now are must have been produced out of nothing, absolutely and without a cause, which is a plain contradiction in terms. For, to say a thing

is produced and yet that there is no cause at all for that production, is to say
that something is effected by nothing, that is, at the same time when it is not
effected at all. (Clarke 1705, 18–19)

At the core of this line of reasoning is the idea that nothing comes from nothing.
To say that something began to exist without a cause is taken to be contradictory
in the sense that it contradicts the obvious truth that if something begins to exist
it must have a cause.

Proposition (3) says that the thing spoken of in proposition (1) must also exist
necessarily. To exist "necessarily," for Clarke, involves existing on the basis of
something "in the nature of the thing itself," and is synonymous with "self-
existing" (Clarke 1705, 27–28). The supplementary reasoning for this proposition goes as follows:

> For whatever exists must either have come into being out of nothing, abso-
> lutely without cause, or it must have been produced by some external cause,
> or it must be self-existent. Now to arise out of nothing absolutely without any
> cause has been already shown to be a plain contradiction. To have been
> produced by some external cause cannot possibly be true of every thing,
> but something must have existed eternally and independently, as has likewise
> been shown already. Which remains, therefore, [is] that that being which has
> existed independently from eternity must of necessity be self-existent.
> (Clarke 1705, 27)

This reasoning involves once again the idea that nothing can come from
nothing. Since it has been concluded in proposition (1) that there exists something eternal, it follows that this thing could not have come into being from
nothing, nor could it have an external cause; accordingly, its reason for existence must lie in its own nature.

Proposition (8) is considered by Clarke as decisive, for without (8) one could
grant (1) and (3) but go on to maintain that the eternally existing necessary
existence is something mindless rather than intelligent, and hence not identical
to God. The starting-point of Clarke's reasoning for this proposition is the idea that

> it is impossible that any effect should have any perfection which was not in
> the cause. For if it had, then that perfection would be caused by nothing,
> which is a plain contradiction. (Clarke 1705, 104)

The basic idea in this reasoning is that an effect cannot possess properties that its
cause is not capable of generating (i.e., "the cause must always be more
excellent than the effect"; Clarke 1705, 103). The rationale for this idea is the
above-mentioned principle that nothing can come from nothing. Applied to an
eternal and necessary existence, this means that if there are in the world things
that are intelligent, which obviously there are, then the capacity to generate

intelligence must also be possessed by the cause of these intelligent things. In other words, the eternal and necessary existence must be capable of generating intelligence, or, as Clarke puts it, it must possess intelligence to a "higher degree" (Clarke 1705, 108–109).

In a next step, Clarke argues that intelligence cannot be generated by mindless matter. To this effect it is asked whether intelligence is a "distinct quality" apart from mindless matter, or whether, on the contrary, it can be fully explained in terms of mindless matter. Taking mindless matter to be "a composition of unintelligent figure and motion" (Clarke 1705, 106), Clarke reasons that mindless matter cannot explain intelligence, for

> whatever can arise from, or be compounded of, anything is still only those very things of which it was compounded. (Clarke 1705, 114)

Since intelligence is not a composition of unintelligent figure and motion, it must be a quality distinct from unintelligent figure and motion. And if intelligence is a quality distinct from unintelligent figure and motion, then the principle that an effect cannot possess properties that its cause cannot generate yields the conclusion that mindless matter cannot generate intelligence.

Since mindless matter cannot generate intelligence, it follows that the eternal and necessary existence cannot be mindless matter. It must instead be something capable of generating intelligence. In Clarke's terminology, it must be something possessing intelligence to a higher degree.

4.2 Are Causeless Effects Impossible?

Turning now to Hume's criticisms of Clarke's argument, we start with his objection to (1), the claim that something has existed from eternity. Clarke's reasoning for (1) relied on the principle that nothing can come from nothing. Hume takes issue with this principle, not on the ground that it is false, but on the ground that it is not known to be true.

Hume's contention that we do not know that nothing can come from nothing is put forth already in *Treatise* 1.3.3, and is closely related to his much-discussed skepticism about any alleged knowledge of necessary connections between causes and effects. Hume contends that our idea of an effect is independent of our idea of a cause; there might indeed be a cause of a given effect, even of every effect, but this is not something that is either intuitive or demonstrable.

To support that it is not "intuitive" that an effect must have a cause, Hume suggests four criteria of intuitiveness in *Treatise* 1.3.1 and 1.3.3, which he offers without much elaboration: a claim is intuitive if it is grounded in "resemblance" (e.g., that two humans resemble each other more than a human resembles a fish), "proportions in quantity or number" (e.g., that "two and two" equal "four"), "degrees in quality" (e.g., that a given shade of blue is stronger or weaker than another shade of blue), and "contrariety" (e.g., that something cannot both exist and not exist) (Hume 1739, 142–143, 125–127). Hume holds that it is not intuitive by any of these criteria that an effect must have a cause, and so rejects this claim, at least until some other standard of intuitiveness is found that yields a different result (Hume 1739, 142–143).

In arguing that it is not "demonstrable" that an effect must have a cause, Hume says in *Treatise* 1.3.3 that

> as all distinct ideas are separable from each other, and as the ideas of cause and effect are evidently distinct, 'twill be easy for us to conceive any object to be non-existent this moment, and existent the next, without conjoining to it the distinct idea of a cause or productive principle. The separation, therefore, of the idea of a cause from that of a beginning of existence, is plainly possible for the imagination; and consequently the actual separation of these objects is so far possible, that it implies no contradiction nor absurdity; and is therefore incapable of being refuted by any reasoning from mere ideas; without which 'tis impossible to demonstrate the necessity of a cause. (Hume 1739, 143)

As can be seen, the conceptual independence of an effect from a cause is here used as a basis for concluding that we cannot demonstrate that every effect has a ground for its existence.

As far as intuition and demonstration go, Hume deems it an open question whether effects can begin to exist without prior causes. But might there be any other way to decide the matter apart from intuition and demonstration?

In his short pamphlet *A Letter from a Gentleman to His Friend in Edinburgh* (1745), written in defense of the *Treatise*, Hume suggests that the question of causeless effects is to be decided on grounds of what he calls "moral evidence," a distinct kind of certainty not further explained. Hume says that in the *Treatise* he took

> the Freedom of disputing the common Opinion, that it [i.e., the causal principle] was founded on demonstrative or intuitive Certainty; but asserts, that it is supported by moral Evidence ... (Hume 1967, 22)

However, in his next book, the *Enquiry*, Section XII, the question of causeless effects is now taken to be a question to be settled by experience:

> The existence, therefore, of any being can only be proved by arguments from its cause or its effect; and these arguments are founded entirely on experience. If we reason a priori, anything may appear able to produce anything. (Hume 1748, 254)

That Hume thinks humans lack experience of the relevant kind is clear from his analysis of causation as solely a constant conjunction between events, with no mention of any necessary connections. Since we do not experience necessary connections, we cannot infer from any effect that it *must* have a cause. The possibility of a causeless effect is accordingly left open.

In the *Dialogues*, Hume extends this basic line of reasoning to support not just the supposition that the universe viewed as a contingent whole need not have a cause beyond itself, but also to support the further supposition that the universe viewed as a chain or series of infinite contingent causes need not have a necessary cause beyond itself either. For if causeless effects are possible, there is no need to seek a necessary cause beyond the chain of infinite contingent causes either, and so the chain can be supposed "sufficiently explained in explaining the cause of the parts" (Hume 1779, 167).

Against Hume's allowance of causeless effects it has in recent times been urged that Hume is employing a different standard of intuitive knowledge than Clarke. In basing knowledge of the causal principle on "intuition," Clarke means that we know this principle a priori, by just understanding it (Rowe 1975, 82). Hume rejects this standard of intuitiveness, however, and this is crucial to his unwillingness to grant the principle. If this is correct, it would seem that at the root of Hume's objection is a different foundational belief as to what should count as intuitive knowledge, which in turn indicates a radically different epistemological starting-point.

4.3 Is "Necessary Existence" a Coherent Notion?

Turning next to Hume's objection to proposition (3), the claim that the eternal existence must also exist necessarily, it may be recalled that Clarke's reasoning for this proposition involves the principle that nothing can come from nothing. For this reason Hume's objection to (1) carries over also to (3). But Hume has a further objection to (3), which he articulates in Dialogue IX, according to which the very idea of a necessary existence is contradictory. The objection goes as follows:

> Nothing is demonstrable, unless the contrary implies a contradiction. Nothing, that is distinctly conceivable, implies a contradiction. Whatever we conceive as existent, we can also conceive as non-existent. There is no being, therefore, whose non-existence implies a contradiction. / It is pretended that the Deity is a necessarily existent being; and this necessity of his existence is attempted to be explained by asserting, that if we knew his whole essence or nature, we should perceive it to be as impossible for him not to exist, as for twice two not to be four. But it is evident that this can never happen, while our faculties remain the same as at present. It will still be possible for us, at any time, to conceive the non-existence of what we formerly conceived to exist; nor can the mind ever lie

under a necessity of supposing any object to remain always in being; in the same manner as we lie under a necessity of always conceiving twice two to be four. The words, therefore, necessary existence, have no meaning; or, which is the same thing, none that is consistent. (Hume 1779, 163)

Hume is here assuming that whatever is conceivable is also possible, since nothing conceivable involves a contradiction and nothing that does not involve a contradiction is impossible. Granting that the non-existence of anything is conceivable, Hume is accordingly led to conclude that the nonexistence of God is also possible, and hence that God's existence is not necessary. From this it follows that if one were to maintain that God is a necessary being, one would implicitly be maintaining both that God's existence is necessary and that it is not necessary, which of course is a contradiction.

Against Hume's objection it has in recent times been replied that Hume is here taking the proposition that something exists "necessarily" as meaning that its existence could not consistently be denied "no matter what the premises [are]," and accordingly that its necessity can, as it were, be conceived "in a mental vacuum" (Stewart 1985, 251, 252). This is said to be at variance with what Clarke meant; Clarke's conclusion that something exists necessarily means rather that "in relation to a prescribed sequence of thought," namely the premises from which Clarke's reasoning proceeds, it follows that something exists necessarily, since "you cannot consistently reject the conclusion of a demonstration if you accept its premises" (Stewart 1985, 251, 252). If this is right, Hume's objection would seem to involve "a logical blunder" (Stewart 1985, 254). J. C. A. Gaskin has taken issue with this assessment, however. Hume indicates at the beginning of the above quoted passage that by "necessary" he takes Clarke to mean "demonstrable," where something is demonstrable if it follows from "a valid argument from necessarily true premises," where a premise is in turn necessarily true if it cannot be denied without contradiction (Gaskin 1988, 77). Hume appears to have had this sense of "necessary" in view in discussing Clarke's argument rather than the sense imputed by Stewart. If so, Hume and Clarke appear to agree that if a necessary existence is to be an object of knowledge it needs to follow from premises which cannot be denied without contradiction. Clarke's supplementary reasoning makes clear that he does in fact think that (3) cannot be denied without contradiction, since it follows from the supposition that nothing can come from nothing, and this, Clarke thinks, cannot be denied without contradiction. Hume, by contrast, thinks that (3) can be denied without contradiction, precisely because he denies that it can be said to be known that nothing comes from nothing. This suggests that the real point of contention between Hume and Clarke reduces to a disagreement over whether we know that nothing comes from nothing.

4.4 Couldn't Matter Cause Mind?

Hume's objection to proposition (8), the claim that the eternally existing necessary being has intelligence, takes issue with two key assumptions in Clarke's supporting reasoning for this proposition, namely that an effect cannot have a property that its cause is not capable of producing, and that mindless matter is not capable of producing intelligence. Hume objects to both of these assumptions.

Against the assumption that an effect cannot have a property that its cause is not capable of producing, Hume invokes his above-discussed skepticism about necessary connections between causes and effects. Says Hume in *Enquiry* XII:

> If we reason a priori, anything may appear able to produce anything. The falling of a pebble may, for aught we know, extinguish the sun; or the wish of a man control the planets in their orbits. It is only experience, which teaches us the nature and bounds of cause and effect, and enables us to infer the existence of one object from that of another.* (Hume 1748, 254)

In a footnote he adds:

> * That impious maxim of the ancient philosophy, *Ex nihilo, nihil fit* [i.e., from nothing comes nothing], by which the creation of matter was excluded, ceases to be a maxim, according to this philosophy. Not only the will of the supreme Being may create matter; but, for aught we know *a priori*, the will of any other being might create it, or any other cause, that the most whimsical imagination can assign. (Hume 1748, 254)

If it is unknown whether effects must have causes, then the supposition that an effect cannot have a property that its cause is not capable of producing will be equally unknown. The upshot is that as far as our knowledge is concerned, any sort of effect could be caused equally by anything or by nothing at all. It would be up to experience to tell us what is the case.

Against Clarke's further assumption that mindless matter is not capable of producing intelligence, it would be natural to expect Hume to once again invoke skepticism about necessary connections between causes and effects: if it is an open question whether an effect needs to be caused by something capable of producing all the properties of the effect, then it is also an open question whether intelligence can be produced by mindless matter. However, Hume chooses a different style of criticism when it comes to this assumption. Discussing this in Dialogue IX, he says:

> [W]hy may not the material universe be the necessarily existent Being, according to this pretended explication of necessity? We dare not affirm that we know all the qualities of matter; and for aught we can determine, it may contain some qualities, which, were they known, would make its non-existence appear as great a contradiction as that twice two is five. (Hume 1779, 164–165)

So instead of arguing that mindless matter could, as far as we know, be able to produce intelligence, Hume grants the relevant causal principle and instead holds that there might be properties in matter that are unknown to us and which are capable of producing intelligence.

In recent discussions, the above aspect of Hume's criticism of Clarke's argument is rarely brought up for extensive discussion (see, e.g., Gaskin 1988; Yandell 1990; Bailey and O'Brien 2014). This might be because the soundness of the criticism boils down to whether matter can produce intelligence, and this, of course, is a major topic in its own right in contemporary philosophy of mind, quite independently of any cosmological argument. To adequately address this aspect of Hume's criticisms would accordingly require a daunting digression into a separate and contentious field of philosophy.

5 Arguments from Design

The design argument comes in a variety of different versions. Sometimes it is presented as an inference from orderliness in nature to an underlying intelligence as the explanation for this order. At other times, the argument is presented as an inference from purposefulness in nature to an underlying intelligence as the explanation of this purposefulness. Both of these versions of the argument have in turn often been put into the form of either straightforward deductive arguments or arguments based on an analogy between the order or purpose of natural phenomena and human artefacts such as clocks. Hume discusses the principal versions of the design argument in both of the above forms, although without pointing out in any systematic fashion that he is now discussing the argument under this or that particular version.

5.1 The Targeted Argument in Outline

Hume's criticisms of the design argument are difficult to pin to any particular proponent of the argument. Various candidates have been proposed in the literature, including Joseph Butler, George Berkeley, and Isaac Newton (see Hurlbutt 1965 for the standard study of some main proposals). There is even reason to think that Hume might not have any particular proponent of the design argument in mind, for in a letter from 1751 discussing the design argument of the *Dialogues* Hume says that he wishes the argument "cou'd be so analys'd as to be render'd quite formal and regular" (Greig 1932, 155). This clearly indicates a wish for a more specific version of the argument which in turn suggests that he was operating with a rather unspecific version of the argument in the *Dialogues*.

Despite difficulties in pinning Hume's treatment of the design argument to any particular proponent, the argument is still articulated with a sensitivity to its different forms. A design argument from *natural orderliness* is presented in *Enquiry* XI:

> The religious philosophers [. . .] paint, in the most magnificent colours, the order, beauty, and wise arrangement of the universe; and then ask, if such a glorious display of intelligence could proceed from the fortuitous concourse of atoms, or if chance could produce what the greatest genius can never sufficiently admire. (Hume 1748, 210)

A design argument from *natural purposefulness* is developed by Cleanthes in Dialogue II:

> The curious adapting of means to ends, throughout all nature, resembles exactly, though it much exceeds, the productions of human contrivance; of human designs, thought, wisdom, and intelligence. Since, therefore, the effects resemble each other, we are led to infer, by all the rules of analogy, that the causes also resemble; and that the Author of Nature is somewhat similar to the mind of man, though possessed of much larger faculties, proportioned to the grandeur of the work which he has executed. By this argument a posteriori, and by this argument alone, do we prove at once the existence of a Deity, and his similarity to human mind and intelligence. (Hume 1779, 47–48)

The above argument from purposefulness is also an *argument from analogy*, as it is based on a presumed analogy between human artefacts and natural phenomena. Later on, in Dialogue III, Hume has Cleanthes propose a *straightforwardly deductive* form of the argument, an argument that proceeds "immediately" and without appeal to any rules of analogy:

> Consider, anatomize the eye: survey its structure and contrivance; and tell me, from your own feeling, if the idea of a contriver does not immediately flow in upon you with a force like that of sensation. The most obvious conclusion, surely, is in favour of design; and it requires time, reflection, and study, to summon up those frivolous, though abstruse objections, which can support infidelity. (Hume 1779, 77–78)

In scrutinizing the design argument, Hume identifies a set of general problems that strike equally at arguments from natural orderliness and natural purposefulness, as well as a set of more particular problems relating to specific versions of the argument.

5.2 Can Something Unexplained Explain Anything?

An initial worry that Hume's Philo brings up regarding the design argument derives from a sense that something that is in itself unexplained cannot suffice as an explanation of anything. Since the supposed intelligence posited to explain the relevant purposeful structures is left unexplained by the proponent of the design argument, it is sensed that such an intelligence does not suffice as an explanation of the relevant phenomena. Says Philo:

> a mental world, or universe of ideas, requires a cause as much, as does a material world . . . If the material world rests upon a similar ideal world, this ideal world must rest upon some other; and so on, without end. It were better, therefore, never to look beyond the present material world. (Hume 1779, 91–92)

The idea in this passage is that positing an unexplained intelligence to explain the relevant purposeful structures is on a par with positing these structures as mere brute facts.

In response to this initial worry it has been replied that it is unreasonable to require an explanation that it be itself explainable. For example, it would count as a reasonable explanation of Jones's loss of his fortune that the wheel of fortune that he bet on spun in a certain way, even though we might not be able to explain why it is that the wheel spun this way rather than that way (see Swinburne 1991, 73–74). This reply might be generalized over many other explanations: to posit a force of gravity to explain why an apple falls down when let go of, could reasonably count as an "explanation" of the fall of the apple even in the absence of an explanation of the force of gravity itself, for example.

5.3 Need the Intelligence Be Infinite or Perfect?

A further set of problems concern the validity of inferring a "divine" intelligence from natural orderliness or purposefulness. In Dialogue V, Hume has Philo draw attention to various attributes typically ascribed to the divine, including various "infinite" and "perfect" attributes. The natural phenomena from which the inference of an intelligence proceed do not require us to infer that the intelligence that underlies these phenomena, even if such an intelligence is granted, has any attributes to an infinite or perfect degree; it would be equally consistent with the phenomena for this intelligence to be finite and imperfect. Says Philo:

> *First*, By this method of reasoning, you renounce all claim to infinity in any of the attributes of the Deity. [. . .] *Secondly*, You have no reason, on your theory, for ascribing perfection to the Deity, even in his finite capacity, or for supposing him free from every error, mistake, or incoherence, in his undertakings. (Hume 1779, 104–105)

The inference of an intelligence rests on the principle that a given effect can be explained by reference to a cause whose properties can explain the properties found in the effect: if the effect consists in a purposeful arrangement, then the cause needs to be capable of conferring purpose; and so on. Hume's point is that to have the capacity to arrange things purposefully does not require possessing these capacities to an infinite or perfect degree.

Against Hume's criticism it has been objected in recent times that it runs counter to reasonable scientific methodology to require that a cause possess only those properties that are needed to explain the properties of its effect. According to Swinburne, this requirement would be tantamount to requiring that all that can be said about the cause of an effect is that it has effect-producing characteristics, which "would not add an iota to our knowledge" (Swinburne 1963, 207). In defense of Hume, it might be said that what he is objecting to is the belief that natural orderliness or purposefulness *must* have its origin in an infinite and perfect intelligence, which, of course, does not imply that it could not have such an origin or that it would conflict with a reasonable scientific methodology to posit such an origin as a hypothetical possibility.

5.4 Need There Be Just One Intelligence?

A further general problem with the design argument that Hume points out is that there is nothing about natural orderliness or purposefulness that implies that there can be only one single intelligence behind these phenomena. It would be just as consistent with the relevant phenomena for there to be a plurality of intelligences, just as it is often the case that human artefacts are the product of a group of people rather than just one person. Says Philo:

> And what shadow of an argument, continued PHILO, can you produce, from your hypothesis, to prove the unity of the Deity? A great number of men join in building a house or ship, in rearing a city, in framing a commonwealth; why may not several deities combine in contriving and framing a world? This is only so much greater similarity to human affairs. (Hume 1779, 107–108)

The possibility of a plurality of intelligences poses a problem for anyone who thinks that the relevant phenomena provide an argument for the existence of a single intelligence.

Against Hume's above reasoning it has been objected in recent times that it can still be reasonable to suppose that the universe is structured by just one intelligence since the laws of nature are uniform throughout the whole universe. If the universe were the product of a plurality of intelligences, "we should expect to find an inverse square law of gravitation obeyed in one part of the universe, and in another part a law which was just short of being an inverse square law" (Swinburne 1963, 210). To this it might be replied that what Hume principally seems to be objecting to is the belief that natural orderliness or purposefulness *must* have its origin in one single intelligence, which, of course, does not preclude that this could in fact be the case.

5.5 Is the Analogy Strong Enough?

A further problem that Hume identifies is concerned specifically with the analogical version of the design argument. The idea on which the analogical version of the argument is based is that the intelligence that we know from experience is present in the causes of human artefacts can reasonably be supposed to be present also in the cause of the relevant natural phenomena, since these phenomena bear a resemblance to human artefacts in regard to orderliness and purposefulness.

Against this Hume has Philo object that the resemblance that we know from experience to obtain between natural orderliness or purposefulness and human artefacts could equally be said to obtain between these phenomena and various other sorts of causes. For example, the cause of the relevant natural phenomena could reasonably be supposed to resemble a plant, for we know from experience that natural phenomena such as apples, carrots, and flowers are caused by other plants further up in the plant genealogy. Again, the cause of the relevant natural phenomena could reasonably be supposed to resemble an animal, for we know from experience that animals are caused by other animals further up in the animal genealogy. Says Philo:

> The world plainly resembles more an animal or a vegetable, than it does a watch or a knitting-loom. Its cause, therefore, it is more probable, resembles the cause of the former. The cause of the former is generation or vegetation. The cause, therefore, of the world, we may infer to be something similar or analogous to generation or vegetation. [. . .] [D]oes not a plant or an animal, which springs from vegetation or generation, bear a stronger resemblance to the world, than does any artificial machine, which arises from reason and design? (Hume 1779, 131–132)

Since a plant or animal would be something quite different from a divine intelligence, it would seem to follow that the analogical reasoning used in the design argument is equally consistent with the inference of a cause other than a divine intelligence.

A related problem with the argument is that if it were granted that a divine intelligence is the cause of natural orderliness and purposefulness insofar as human intelligence can reasonably be supposed to be the cause of orderly and purposeful human artefacts, then by this same logic there is no reason not to suppose that the supposed divine intelligence inhabits a physical body with a face, eyes, nose, hair, and so on, since the intelligent human minds that are the causes of human artefacts inhabit physical bodies with these sorts of properties. Says Philo:

> And why not become a perfect Anthropomorphite? Why not assert the deity or deities to be corporeal, and to have eyes, a nose, mouth, ears, &c.? (Hume 1779, 110)

Since proponents of the design argument do not typically conceive of the divine intelligence as having physical properties such as eyes, nose, hair, and so on, it would seem that their conception of the divine intelligence is inconsistent with the type of analogical reasoning which the logic of this argument would equally support.

Against Hume's above reasoning it has been objected in recent times that there is a significant difference between properties such as intelligence on the one hand and bodily or facial features on the other, for whereas the former play an important role in explaining the relevant natural phenomena, bodily, or facial features do not play any such explanatory role (see Swinburne 1963, 209). A possible counter to this might be that from Hume's empiricist point of view all our knowledge of causes is grounded in experience, and since the intelligent causes of which we have actual experience are all embodied, it is reasonable, and by no means arbitrary, to suppose that a divine intelligence would be similarly embodied.

Adding to the above, it is also worth pointing out that Hume also has Philo insist that the strength of the analogical version of the design argument is wholly proportionate to the presumed resemblance between the orderliness and purposefulness of human artefacts and the orderliness or purposefulness of natural phenomena, where the degree of resemblance is something we can know only from experience:

> The exact similarity of the cases gives us a perfect assurance of a similar event; and a stronger evidence is never desired nor sought after. But wherever you depart, in the least, from the similarity of the cases, you diminish proportionably the evidence; and may at last bring it to a very weak analogy, which is confessedly liable to error and uncertainty. (Hume 1779, 49–50)

Hume goes on to say that the resemblance appealed to in the design argument is highly uncertain. For whereas we have experience of the origination of human artefacts, allowing us to infer that their causes have intelligence, we lack any corresponding experience of the cause of the relevant natural phenomena, leaving us unable to ascertain the extent of the resemblance:

> [S]urely you will not affirm, that the universe bears such a resemblance to a house, that we can with the same certainty infer a similar cause, or that the analogy is here entire and perfect. The dissimilitude is so striking, that the utmost you can here pretend to is a guess, a conjecture, a presumption concerning a similar cause . . . (Hume 1779, 51)

We have no experience of the formation of the relevant natural phenomena. Accordingly, we have no ground for saying that these phenomena bear a strong resemblance to human artefacts, and so we end up with an analogy which might, for all we know, be very weak, leading to mere conjecture rather than to any solid conclusion (Hume 1779, 69–70).

Against this reasoning it has in recent times been objected that there is no need to have experience of the formation of universes in order to arrive at knowledge of what their cause is. Referring to modern cosmology, Swinburne points out that "cosmologists are reaching very well-tested scientific conclusions about the Universe as a whole" (Swinburne 1963, 208). A possible reply to this might be offered on the basis of Hume's reasoning in *Enquiry* IV, according to which any purported knowledge of matters beyond our immediate experience, including of the history of the universe, would depend on knowing that the laws of nature are uniform across time, which is something that we have no experience of (Hume 1748, 47–68). If this is right, then what counts as knowledge of the history of the universe in modern cosmology would fall short of being knowledge in Hume's sense.

5.6 What about Naturalistic Alternatives?

A final problem, attaching specifically to the design argument from purposefulness, concerns the possibility of explaining the perceived purposefulness of the relevant natural phenomena in a way that renders the purposefulness merely apparent, not real. This could be done by sketching a naturalistic scenario in which the relevant natural phenomena emerged entirely from natural causes devoid of any intentionality. Such a scenario would ensure that what is perceived as purposeful in nature is only purposeful in appearance, not in reality, since there is no intentionality to confer purpose on anything.

Hume sketches a naturalistic scenario of this sort in Dialogue VIII. Posit a finite number of particles moving around and colliding with each other in space by virtue of blind, unguided forces. It will then be the case that

> A finite number of particles is only susceptible of finite transpositions: and it must happen, in an eternal duration, that every possible order or position must be tried an infinite number of times. This world, therefore, with all its events, even the most minute, has before been produced and destroyed, and will again be produced and destroyed, without any bounds and limitations. No one, who has a conception of the powers of infinite, in comparison of finite, will ever scruple this determination. (Hume 1779, 146–147)

To this scenario, Hume adds the proto-Darwinian idea that where a particular configuration allows for "constancy in forms" (i.e., is biologically well adapted), the result will be "the same appearance of art and contrivance which we observe at present" (Hume 1779, 149). This hypothesis is not only logically possible but, even has a "faint appearance of probability" (Hume 1779, 146).

If Hume's naturalistic scenario is granted as logically possible, it will suffice to undermine any straightforward deduction of an intelligence behind the relevant natural phenomena, as any such deduction would require that it is impossible that the relevant natural phenomena exist while an underlying intelligence does not.

Against Hume's above reasoning it has been objected that the unlikeliness of the relevant naturalistic scenario is proportionate to "the amount of order to be accounted for," and that the amount of order in the universe happens to be "very striking" (Swinburne 1963, 211). In response it might be said that Hume's point is not that the naturalistic scenario is likely, but that it is logically possible, in which case at least any straightforward deduction of a divine intelligence from natural phenomena – such as the "immediate" deduction Cleanthes proposes in Dialogue III – will be invalidated.

6 Arguments from Miracles

Arguments from miracles were among the most debated kinds of religious arguments in Hume's day (see Burns 1981 for the standard account of these debates). It is accordingly not surprising that this type of argument is the topic of one of Hume's earliest essays, "Of Miracles," which appeared for the first time as Section X of the *Enquiry* but which we know from Hume's correspondence was written much earlier, at the same time as the *Treatise* (Greig 1932, 25). In this early essay, Hume offers a famous critique of miracle arguments, a critique which takes aim at "all kinds of superstitious Delusion" but is applied in particular to arguments in support of "the Christian Religion" (Hume 1748, 174, 203).

6.1 The Targeted Argument in Outline

Arguments from miracles were used to support Christian doctrines in the work of prominent seventeenth- and eighteenth-century English philosophers such as Robert Boyle, John Locke, and Samuel Clarke. According to Clarke,

> The Christian Revelation is positively and directly proved . . . by the many infallible Signs and Miracles, which the Author of it worked publickly as the Evidence of his Divine Commission. (Clarke 1706, 346–347)

Locke says similarly, with reference to the miracles of Jesus Christ, that

> where the miracle is admitted, the doctrine cannot be rejected; it comes with the assurance of a divine attestation to him that allows the miracle, and he cannot question its truth. (Locke 1743, 9)

Boyle agrees, saying that what makes us "sufficiently ascertained" of Christian doctrines are "the miracles wrought by Christ" (Boyle 1772, 531).

The core structure in the reasonings of the above writers is rarely stated systematically, but it might be useful to do so here to help us see what exactly Hume is objecting to. The core structure in these reasonings is roughly as follows:

(1) Christian doctrine is based on the teachings of Jesus Christ.
(2) To make the truth of his teachings evident, Jesus Christ performed various miracles which he would not have been able to perform if he were not credible.
(3) These miracles have been reliably reported by the first Christian community, and recorded in the New Testament.
(4) Hence, we have reliable grounds for believing the teachings of Jesus Christ. (From 2 and 3.)
(5) Hence, we have reliable grounds for believing Christian doctrine. (From 1 and 4.)

If we take Christian doctrine to include what we in this study are calling "traditional Christian theism," the above argument will be seen to contain an implicit argument for the existence of an infinitely powerful, knowledgeable, and good God.

6.2 Hume's Objection

To understand the gist of Hume's objection, we do well to take into account what he presents as its main conclusion. The main conclusion is foreshadowed at the beginning of Hume's discussion in these words:

> I have discover'd an Argument ... which, if just, will, with the Wise and Learned, be an everlasting Check to all Kinds of superstitious Delusion. (Hume 1748, 174)

At the end of his discussion, the conclusion is stated explicitly:

> we may conclude, that the *Christian Religion* not only was at first attended with Miracles, but even at this Day cannot be believed by any reasonable Person without one. (Hume 1748, 203)

Assuming that by reasonability Hume means rationality, the conclusion of Hume's argument is that it is irrational to believe in miracle reports such as those purporting to support of Christian doctrine. Hume's objection is accordingly directed at premise (3) of the above argument; his contention is that it is irrational to recognize any *reliable* reports for the miracles of Jesus Christ.

To understand how Hume arrives at this conclusion, we need to know how he understands rationality, evidence, and miracles. He explains this in Part I of

Enquiry X. With regard to rationality, his central idea is that a rational person "proportions his Belief to the Evidence" (Hume 1748, 175). This leads directly to the question what is meant by "evidence." The sort of evidence that Hume recognizes must derive from experience, although this experience may reach us via the testimony of others. Hume goes on to distinguish between two kinds of experience, *constant* experience, which is what we have when an event is always followed by another event, and *variable* experience, which we have when an event is sometimes followed by another event but not always (Hume 1748, 174–175).

Since a rational person proportions belief to evidence, it follows that if there is a clash between their constant experience and someone's testimony contravening that experience, the rational person will always reject the testimony. For example, if my experience says that there is a constant conjunction between a body dying and that body decaying, and someone tells me that they have seen a body die but not decay but instead come back to life, then reason would require of me that I reject their report unless I have an equally constant experience of the truth of testimony.

If we define "laws of nature" as regularities backed up by constant experience, and "miracles" as events contravening laws of nature (as does Hume 1748, 180–181), we can express the above point by saying that a rational person will always reject a miracle report *unless* the reliability of that report is experienced with equal constancy (Hume 1748, 182). This is the thrust of Part I of *Enquiry* X.

In Part II of *Enquiry* X, Hume goes on to argue that we are not in a position to say that a miracle report could be backed up by constant experience, on at least four grounds. First, because we know from experience that people can sometimes be deluded or deceitful (Hume 1748, 183). Second, because we know from experience that people can sometimes be swayed by a love of wonder into believing that things happened otherwise than they actually happened (Hume 1748, 184). Third, because we know from experience that not all people have reliable standards for belief formation (Hume 1748, 186). And fourth, because we know from experience that reports of miracles have been put forth in support of incompatible religious claims, meaning that some of these reports must certainly be false (Hume 1748, 190).

Taking the four above considerations into account, Hume is led to deny that we have anything like constant experience backing up miracle reports. But since we do have constant experience of laws of nature, it follows that a rational person will not concede a miracle report. Accordingly, the reports of the early Christian community recorded in the New Testament as to the miracles of Jesus Christ are not considered reliable. And so the argument from miracles collapses.

6.3 Do Miracles Contravene Constant Experience or Laws of Nature?

Hume's objection to the argument from miracles drew a large amount of critical responses from his contemporaries (see Tweyman 1996 for an overview of early responses), and has continued to draw critical responses down to the present day. In what follows, I give a sampling of critical responses, old and new, along with some replies.

In Hume's day George Campbell's *A Dissertation on Miracles* (1762) was widely regarded as one of the most important critical responses to Hume's objection. Campbell, in turn, considered Hume's objection "one of the most dangerous attacks that have been made on our religion" (Campbell 1762, vi).

Of Campbell's various responses to Hume's reasoning, one of the most noteworthy is his claim that there is strictly speaking no such thing as constant experience of laws of nature. Campbell's reasoning is as follows. What we call laws of nature are generalizations from experience, but what we experience is always something particular and hence is always different from case to case. If I yesterday experienced that A was followed by B, and today experience that A is followed by B, I have not experienced one and the same thing, but different things, and I only take them to be an experience of a common law of nature by a process of generalization. Accordingly, if there is no constant experience backing up laws of nature, we are not entitled to say, as Hume does, that a miracle report conflicts with constant experience (Campbell 1762, 33).

In more recent times, Larmer (2014) has developed a response that overlaps somewhat with Campbell's. Larmer's basic contention is that "*a priori* in-principle dismissals of the possibility or probability of justified belief in miracles fail" (Larmer 2014, 187). He takes the flaw of Hume's reasoning to lie in the claim that miracles must be defined as violations of laws of nature. We can see that this claim is incorrect, he says, by "reflecting on the fact that the laws of nature do not themselves allow the predication or explanation of any event" (Larmer 2014, 38). Larmer provides an example of such a reflection:

> It is, for example, impossible to predict what will happen on a billiard table by making reference solely to Newton's laws of motion. One must also make reference to the number of balls on the table, their initial position, the condition of the felt, the angle the cue stick is held at, and so on. (Larmer 2014, 39)

Larmer takes these reflections to validate a "basic distinction" between "the laws of nature" and "the stuff of nature," the latter being "the material conditions to which the laws of nature apply" (Larmer 2014, 39). This distinction enables Larmer to say that God can perform miracles by changing material conditions in the world, for example by creating or annihilating units of energy or by causing such units to occupy different places. For example,

> if God were to create *ex nihilo* a spermatozoon which fertilized an egg in the body of a virgin no laws of nature would be broken, yet the usual course of nature would have been overridden in such a way as to bring about an event nature would not otherwise have produced. (Larmer 2014, 39)

If this approach makes sense, it would mean that a central assumption of Hume's objection is flawed.

An objection to Larmer's response might be that, in taking God to have intervened in the world by creating, annihilating or changing the material conditions of energy, one is *ipso facto* taking God to have violated a law of nature, namely the Principle of Conservation of Energy. Larmer takes this objection to blur the distinction between a "scientific" and a "metaphysical" reading of the relevant law, however. On a scientific reading, the law makes a claim only about the behavior of energy in isolated systems, whereas on a metaphysical reading it makes a claim about reality in its totality (Larmer 2014, 41). On the scientific reading, the law cannot properly be taken to be violated by divine intervention in the world, for such intervention entails that the world is no longer viewed as an isolated system (Larmer 2014, 41–46).

6.4 Does Hume's Objection Involve Circular Reasoning?

A very common response to Hume's objection to miracle arguments takes the objection to involve circular reasoning. Lewis (1947) famously urges one version of this response as follows:

> Now of course we must agree with Hume that if there is absolutely "uniform experience" against miracles, if in other words they have never happened, why then they never have. Unfortunately we know the experience against them to be uniform only if we know that all the reports of them are false. And we can know all the reports to be false only if we know already that miracles have never occurred. In fact, we are arguing in a circle. (Lewis 1947, 123)

In more recent times, Johnson (1999) has made a similar case: it could only be said that there is constant experience that all *A*s are *B*s if this or that miracle report saying that some *A* is not a *B* was known to be false, but to claim such knowledge would be to beg the question (Johnson 1999, 18).

Against the above charges, it has been replied that the point of Hume's reasoning is not that the experience behind the laws of nature is known to be constant to the exclusion of any contravening phenomena, but rather that the nature of the testimony in support of miracles is tainted on account of the various factors mentioned in Part II of *Enquiry* X: the possibility of deceit, delusion, low standards for belief formation, and things of this sort (Fogelin 2005, 37–38).

6.5 Is Hume's Objection Based on a Flawed Probability Principle?

Another recent response to Hume's objection is found in Earman (2000). Earman holds that Hume's claim that since all the As we experience are Bs we have a constant experience that all As are Bs, translates to a probabilistic principle which Earman calls "Hume's straight rule of induction": "If n As have been examined, all of which were found to be Bs, then if n is sufficiently large, the probability that all As are Bs is 1" (Earman 2000, 22). This principle, says Earman, is both crude and at odds with scientific practice:

> Among the zillions of protons observed by particle physicists, none has been verified to decay. But particle physicists do not assign a probability of 1 to the proposition that the next proton to be observed will not decay, and they certainly do not think that they have adequate inductive grounds for probabilistic certainty with respect to the general proposition that no proton ever decays – otherwise the expenditure of time and money on experiments to detect proton decay would be inexplicable on standard expected utility model of decision making. (Earman 2000, 31)

In defending Hume against Earman, Fogelin grants that "Hume's straight rule of induction" is flawed, but he denies that there is any good reason for supposing that Hume's objection makes use of this principle. That all the As that have been experienced are Bs does indeed mean that constant experience supports that all As are Bs, but this does not imply that the probability of this relation between A and B is 1, nor, conversely, that the probability that A is not B is 0. And not only is no such thing implied, but Hume does not even need such an implication for his argument to work (see Fogelin 2005, 45–53).

7 Arguments from Evil

Taking himself to have shown that the traditional Christian claim that there exists an infinitely powerful, knowledgeable and good God is lacking in rational demonstration, Hume next turns his attention to showing that traditional Christian theism lacks coherent meaning. This is done in connection with his discussion of the problem of evil in Dialogues X and XI.

Throughout Dialogues X and XI Hume argues that the occurrence of evil in the world precludes the possibility of inferring the existence of a good and benevolent God. And in a famous and key passage in Dialogue X he argues that the occurrence of evil is incompatible with a good and benevolent God. I shall call Hume's line of reasoning on the first point his inference argument, and his line of reasoning on the second point his incompatibility argument.

The more serious challenge to traditional Christian theism is clearly the incompatibility argument. For even if the inference argument were unanswerable, all that would follow is that the existence of a good and benevolent God cannot be inferred from phenomena in the natural world. The existence of a good and benevolent God would remain untouched. Things look differently with the incompatibility argument, however: if the challenge posed by this argument turns out to be unanswerable, then the very meaningfulness or coherence of traditional Christian theism will be up for question. I will accordingly devote more attention to Hume's incompatibility argument.

7.1 The Inference Argument

Hume's inference argument aims at showing that the occurrence of evil in the world bars us from inferring that there exists a good and benevolent God behind the order of the world. As Gaskin (1988, 52) points out, the inference argument is really a part of Hume's criticism of the design argument, though it may be singled out as a "special case" since it is concerned not so much with the existence of an intelligence behind the world as with its possession of the attributes of goodness and benevolence.

The operating principle of Hume's inference argument is that it is not reasonable to infer anything about the nature of a cause beyond what is required by the nature of its supposed effect. In the context of the design argument, the world is the supposed effect. But the world contains what Hume calls "mixed phenomena": positive things like joy and happiness, on the one hand, but also negative things like pain and suffering, on the other. The joy and happiness in the world would seem to support the inference of a good and benevolent intelligence behind these phenomena, but the pain and suffering in the world would seem to license either of two contrary conclusions, namely either that the intelligence behind the world possesses both goodness and malice, or else that it possesses neither goodness nor malice. The uniformity of the world leads Hume to favor the latter option:

> There may *four* hypotheses be framed concerning the first causes of the universe: *that* they are endowed with perfect goodness; *that* they have perfect malice; *that* they are opposite, and have both goodness and malice; *that* they have neither goodness nor malice. Mixed phenomena can never prove the two former unmixed principles; and the uniformity and steadiness of general laws seem to oppose the third. The fourth, therefore, seems by far the most probable. (Hume 1779, 221)

Hume is here assuming that a good and benevolent intelligence would ensure a happy and joyful world, whereas an evil or malicious intelligence would ensure the opposite. Hume is also assuming that this world, with its quantity of good and evil, is, at least for purposes of argument, the responsibility of this intelligence.

7.2 The Incompatibility Argument

Hume's incompatibility argument is nested in a discussion pursued throughout most of the *Dialogues* as to the meaningfulness of terms applied to God. In Dialogue II, Hume has Philo maintain that since "we have no experience of divine attributes" we should "beware, lest we think our ideas anywise correspond to his perfections" (Hume 1779, 45). But despite this mismatch between our ideas and God's attributes, Philo holds that we may still "justly ascribe" terms like "Wisdom, Thought, Design, Knowledge" to God inasmuch as "these words are honourable among men" (Hume 1779, 45). In Dialogue III, Hume has Demea articulate a similar position, holding that "none of the materials of thought are in any respect similar in the human and in the divine intelligence," and accordingly that "all our ideas, derived from the senses, are confessedly false and illusive" (Hume 1779, 83). But unlike Philo, Demea concludes from this that it is "unreasonable to transfer such sentiments to a supreme existence" (Hume 1779, 83). In Dialogue IV, Cleanthes pushes back against Demea's conclusion, saying that if our ideas "be not just, and adequate, and correspondent to his real nature," then our beliefs are indistinguishable from those of "Sceptics and Atheists" (Hume 1779, 86). It is largely against this conclusion that Philo pushes back by developing his incompatibility argument in Dialogue X.

Philo's argument unfolds as follows:

> And is it possible, CLEANTHES, said PHILO, that after all these reflections, and infinitely more, which might be suggested, you can still persevere in your Anthropomorphism, and assert the moral attributes of the Deity, his justice, benevolence, mercy, and rectitude, to be of the same nature with these virtues in human creatures? His power we allow infinite: whatever he wills is executed: but neither man nor any other animal are happy: therefore he does not will their happiness. His wisdom is infinite: he is never mistaken in chusing the means to any end: but the course of Nature tends not to human or animal felicity: therefore it is not established for that purpose. Through the whole compass of human knowledge, there are no inferences more certain and infallible than these. In what respect, then, do his benevolence and mercy resemble the benevolence and mercy of men? / EPICURUS'S old questions are yet unanswered. / Is he willing to prevent evil, but not able? then is he impotent. Is he able, but not willing? then is he malevolent. Is he both able and willing? whence then is evil? (Hume 1779, 185–186)

Philo's solution to the problem here outlined, he says, is to regard God's attributes as "incomprehensible"; to understand their nature exceeds both "human capacity" and "common measures of truth and falsehood" (Hume 1779, 188, 194).

But what exactly is the problem that Philo is drawing attention to in the above passage? That he is drawing attention to a contradiction seems plain. But what follows from this contradiction is something about which there is considerable disagreement in the literature. In what follows, I outline a few of the main interpretations.

7.3 Is the Aim to Show that God's Existence Is Unlikely?

A first interpretation, urged by Brian Davies, takes Philo's argument to aim at establishing the *unlikeliness* of God's existence by exhibiting a merely *prima facie* inconsistency between the existence of an almighty and benevolent God and the evil or suffering in the world. Says Davies:

> Philo (and Hume) appear to be saying, that [Cleanthes'] view of God is at odds with the facts of evil. There might, Hume seems to think, be both evil and the God in which Cleanthes believes. But it seems *prima facie* unlikely, and it cannot be proved that there is such a God as the one in which Cleanthes believes. (Davies 2006, 11)

The inconsistency exhibited in Philo's argument is here regarded only as a *prima facie* inconsistency: it results from taking "the simplest" and "most obvious" view of "the phenomena." But, of course, the simplest and most obvious view need not be the correct or only view, and so the inconsistency might be answerable in a number of ways. Evil shows only that God's existence is unlikely, not that it is impossible.

Davies's main reason for taking Philo's argument to be aimed at establishing only an unlikeliness appears to derive from the inference argument urged by Philo mainly in Dialogue XI:

> Discussion of God and evil continues in the *Dialogues* beyond part X . . . [Hume] has Philo conceding that there might be a God even as Cleanthes conceives of him and even though the world is as Philo takes it to be. As the *Dialogues* as a whole makes pretty clear, however, Hume doubts that there is reason to believe in such a God. (Davies 2006, 10)

Given that the inference argument does not call the existence of God into question, Davies is led to think that Philo's argument in Dialogue X should not be regarded as aiming at establishing a real inconsistency between the existence of God and evil, but only a *prima facie* inconsistency which renders God's existence unlikely.

There are problems with this interpretation, however. First, Philo's argument does not terminate in the conclusion that the existence of God is "unlikely," but, rather, that the occurrence of evil in the world can only be accounted for if we take God's attributes to be "incomprehensible." Nowhere in Dialogue X does Philo suggest that his reasoning shows that the existence of God is merely unlikely. Second, this interpretation ignores Philo's announcement at the end of Dialogue X that he will "retire" from his "intrenchment," not because of any lack of confidence in his argument ("I deny that you can ever force me"), but rather for the sake of argument ("What are you advanced by all these concessions?"):

> But I will be contented to retire still from this intrenchment: For I deny that you can ever force me in it: I will allow, that pain or misery is man is *compatible* with infinite power and goodness in the Deity, even in your sense of these attributes: What are you advanced by all these concessions? (Hume 1779, 195)

This announcement makes clear that Philo's inference argument in Dialogue XI is not to be used as the lens through which the incompatibility argument of Dialogue X is to be interpreted. By failing to pay sufficient attention to this, one can be misled into thinking that the argument of Dialogue X continues into Dialogue XI.

7.4 Is the Aim to Show that God's Existence Is Contradictory?

A second interpretation, urged by Nelson Pike, holds that Philo is seeking to show that God does not exist on the grounds that God's existence is inconsistent with the fact of evil. According to Pike,

> Philo argues as follows ... If God is to be all-powerful, all-knowing, and perfectly good (using all key terms in their ordinary sense), then to claim that God exists is to preclude the possibility of admitting that there occur instances of evil; that is, is to preclude the possibility of admitting that there occur instances of suffering, pain, superstition, wickedness, and so forth. The statements "God exists" and "There occur instances of suffering" are logically incompatible. Of course, no one could deny that there occur instances of suffering. Such a denial would plainly conflict with common experience. Thus it follows from obvious fact that God (having the attributes assigned to him by Cleanthes) does not exist. (Pike 1963, 180–181)

Pike develops his interpretation by saying that Philo is claiming that the three propositions "the world contains instances of suffering," "God exists – and is omnipotent and omniscient" and "God exists – and is perfectly good," constitute

an "inconsistent triad" (Pike 1963, 182). To demonstrate that the triad is inconsistent, Pike says that Philo "argues" that "to say of God that he is omnipotent and
omniscient is to say that he *could* prevent suffering if he wanted to," and that "to
say of God that he is perfectly good is to say that God *would* prevent suffering if
he could" (Pike 1963, 182). Pike sums up what he takes to be Philo's contention as
follows:

> "God exists" and "There occur instances of suffering" are logically incom-
> patible statements. Since the latter of these statements is obviously true, the
> former must be false. Philo reflects: "Nothing can shake the solidity of this
> reasoning, so short, so clear (and) so decisive." (Pike 1963, 182)

Pike does not explain how this interpretation follows from Philo's words in
Dialogue X. He offers no exegesis of Philo, nor does he quote the passages
which he takes to exhibit the claims that make up the inconsistent triad. It seems
however that he derives his interpretation from the Epicurus quotes, "Is he
willing to prevent evil, but not able? then is he impotent," and "Is he able, but
not willing? then is he malevolent," along with the question "Whence then is
evil?" which question is suggestive of a contradiction.

There are problems with this interpretation. Pike says Philo concludes his
argument with the phrase "Nothing can shake the solidity of this reasoning, so
short, so clear (and) so decisive," but Pike has here left out the second half of
Philo's conclusion, which runs: " . . . except we assert, that these subjects exceed
all human capacity; and that our common measures of truth and falsehood are
not applicable to them; a topic, which I have all along insisted on." Omitting
this second half of the conclusion gives the impression that Philo is simply
seeking to establish an inconsistency, and therewith the non-existence of God,
whereas taking this part of the conclusion into account suggests that Philo's real
point might be something quite different.

7.5 Is the Aim to Show that "God's Goodness" Lacks Coherent Meaning?

A third interpretation, urged in different forms by Yandell (1990) and myself
(Kraal 2013a), takes the entirety of Philo's conclusion into account. The
contradiction that Philo is seeking to establish between evil and God's goodness
and benevolence serves to show not that God does not exist but rather, as Philo
says, that there is a disanalogy between the meanings of moral terms when
applied to God and humans, a disanalogy that threatens the very meaningfulness
of applications of these terms to God.

In the above quoted key passage, Philo asks Cleanthes if it is possible for him
to maintain "anthropomorphism" in view of the evil in the world. As becomes

clear in the sequel, Philo's question is merely rhetorical; his contention is obviously that anthropomorphism cannot be maintained under these circumstances. But what exactly then is anthropomorphism? This is clarified earlier in the *Dialogues*. From Dialogue II and onwards, Cleanthes is concerned with arguing that the natural order of the world provides reason to infer a being with intelligence, wisdom and power. Demea and Philo worry that this posits an analogy between human and divine attributes that fits ill with the belief that God is incomprehensible, and so in Dialogue IV they accuse Cleanthes of being an "anthropomorphite" (Hume 1779, 48). Although this term is not defined in the *Dialogues*, it is described as the opposite of the view that God's perfections "have any analogy or likeness to the perfections of a human creature" (Hume 1779, 24). This suggests that anthropomorphism, in the *Dialogues*, is the view that there is at least some analogy between human and divine attributes. Since Philo is here concerned specifically with God's moral attributes, the denial of anthropomorphism is in this context a denial of any analogy between human and divine moral attributes.

This denial of any analogy between human and divine moral attributes seems in the *Dialogues* to be tantamount to a semantic claim to the effect that there is no analogy between the meaning of terms such as "good" and "benevolent" when applied to God and humans respectively. Two considerations point strongly to this semantic reading of the argument. First, at the beginning of Dialogue XI Hume has Cleanthes concede Philo's argument by resolving to henceforth use "more accurate and moderate expressions" about God (Hume 1779, 197). And second, after announcing this resolve, Cleanthes goes on to say that "any thing beyond" this reformed usage of expressions leads to "absurdities" (Hume 1779, 197). The "absurdities" here referred to are clearly the absurdities pointed out in Philo's argument, and so what Cleanthes appears to be saying is that Philo's argument leads to a conclusion about the meaning of certain terms when applied to God.

In line with this semantic approach, Yandell proposes the following explication of Philo's argument:

(1) If "good" means the same thing (or something closely analogous) in "God is good" and (say) "Isaiah is good," then God and human persons share the same moral ends (prize the same intrinsic goods).

(2) Humans take their possession of happiness as an intrinsic good – indeed, the highest goal a human person can attain.

(3) In general, human persons are not happy.

(4) God could make all human persons happy, and if He too prized human happiness He would do so.

So: (5) God does not prize human happiness (at least not as the highest good a human person can attain). (*D*, 314)

So: (6) "Good" does not mean the same thing (or something closely analogous) in "God is good" and (say) "Isaiah is good." (1, 2, 5) (Yandell 1990, 246)

Yandell might be overstating Philo's argument, however. What Philo takes to be inconsistent with any even analogical goodness or benevolence in God is not that God does not value human happiness as "the highest goal a human person can attain," but rather that God does not ensure that all humans and animals are "happy." God could fail to ensure that all humans and animals are happy without thereby having to regard it as the highest human goal to attain such happiness, just as God could ensure that all humans and animals are healthy without thereby being committed to taking health to be the highest goal humans and animals can attain.

Having seemingly overstated Philo's argument, Yandell is naturally led to dismiss the argument as question-begging from the point of view of a Christian value-system, where human and animal happiness is not valued as the ultimate goal of human and animal existence (Yandell 1990, 247).

In Kraal (2013a, 585), a modified version of the semantic approach to Philo's argument is developed that replaces the claim that Philo is committed to the assumption that human and animal happiness is the highest attainable goal with the less controversial claim that Philo is committed to the assumption that a good and benevolent God would at least ensure that all humans and animals are happy:

(1) God is almighty, and this entails that everything that happens is willed by God ("His power we allow infinite: whatever he wills is executed").

(2) There are humans and animals that are not happy ("neither man nor any other animal are happy").

(3) Hence it is God's will that some humans and animals are not happy ("therefore he does not will their happiness"). (From 1 and 2.)

(4) If terms expressing God's moral attributes are understandable via analogy to the meanings these terms have when applied to humans, then God's "benevolence" and "mercy" entail that God wills that all human beings and animals are happy.

(5) But God does not will that all humans and animals are happy. (From 3)

(6) Hence it is not the case that God's "benevolence" and "mercy" are understandable via analogy to the meanings these terms have when applied to humans ("is it possible ... [that] the moral attributes of the Deity, his justice, benevolence, mercy, and rectitude, to be of the same nature with these virtues in human creatures?"). (From 4 and 5.)

A crucial assumption in this rendering of the argument would seem to be (4), that is, that in order for terms expressing God's moral attributes to make sense via analogy, ascribing "benevolence" and "mercy" to God would have to imply that God wills all humans and animals to be happy. If Hume is right about this, the theist would definitely be under pressure to explain what they mean in ascribing these terms to God. This challenge will be especially acute if it is granted, as does Hume, that all meaningful terms stand for ideas that derive from sensory impressions, for on this view the only meanings the relevant terms could have would have to be analogical meanings, and so if these terms end up not having analogical meanings it would appear that they do not have meaning at all.

7.6 Impact on Traditional Christian Theism

Assuming that something like the above semantic interpretation of Hume's incompatibility argument does more justice to the actual words of Hume's *Dialogues* than the two rival interpretations, we may next ask what impact this argument has on traditional Christian theism.

The impact on traditional Christian theism depends in large part on whether traditional Christian theism comprises the theological assumptions that the argument, thus interpreted, is predicated on. In particular, it depends on whether traditional Christian theism comprises the doctrine that God's infinite power entails that everything that comes to pass is willed by God (i.e., that "whatever he wills is executed"). Does it?

There is definitely room for discussion on this point. Roman Catholics and Anglicans of Hume's day were typically emphatic about the reality of libertarian free will, which seems to fit ill with this conception of infinite power (see Kraal 2013b for an elaboration of this point). However, if the Presbyterian theology of Hume's immediate Scottish context is taken to reflect the traditional Christian position on what it means for God to have infinite power, then the answer would seem to be Yes. For according to the *Westminster Confession*, "God from all eternity did, by the most wise and holy counsel of his own will, freely and unchangeably ordain whatsoever comes to pass" (Leith 1973, 198). That Hume in the *Dialogues* took this understanding of infinite power to be part and parcel with traditional Christian theism is indicated by his depiction of Philo as "allow-ing" (rather than "arguing") this doctrine in the context of a discussion between the sceptic Philo and his two interlocutors, one of which is the "orthodox" (i.e., orthodox Christian) Demea, without any hint that this might be controversial.

If Hume was right in his seeming assumption that "orthodox" Christian theology, that is, traditional Christian theism, understands the doctrine of infinite power as involving the claim that "whatever he wills is executed," then a consequence of his argument would seem to be that traditional Christian theism lacks coherent meaning. For the ascription of benevolence to God would seem to imply, according to Hume, that God wills all humans and animals to be happy, and the ascription of infinite power to God would seem to imply that God would bring about everything he wills; but it is not the case that all humans and animals are happy. Assuming these things, it is hard to avoid the conclusion that traditional Christian theism lacks coherent meaning.

8 The End Result: A Turn to Hobbesian Theism

As has been noted, the traditional Christian theism of Hume's cultural surrounding took God to be a being with infinite power, knowledge and goodness, and these attributes formed part of what seventeenth- and eighteenth-century philosophers called "the idea of God." We have seen that Hume takes this form of theism to lack both rational demonstration and coherent meaning. In this concluding Section we briefly consider the end result of Hume's thought on these matters: a turn to some form of Hobbesian theism as the only philosophically viable form of theism, that is, the only form of theism that has at least some minimal rational support as well as coherent meaning.

8.1 Hobbesian Themes in Hume's *Dialogues*

If we assume that Hume's *Dialogues* represent the end result of his philosophizing about God, and that Philo by and large represents Hume's thinking in the *Dialogues* (see Section 2.3), we find that there are at least three strong reasons for characterizing Hume's final position as a form of Hobbesian theism.

First, we have seen that Hobbes challenged the idea of God on the ground that we have no ideas of infinite attributes (see Section 3.1). In Dialogue XI, we find that this is precisely the conclusion that Philo forces Cleanthes to draw in response to the incompatibility argument from evil:

> I have been apt to suspect the frequent repetition of the word infinite, which we meet with in all theological writers, to savour more of panegyric than of philosophy; and that any purposes of reasoning, and even of religion, would be better served, were we to rest contented with more accurate and more moderate expressions. The terms, admirable, excellent, superlatively great, wise, and holy; these sufficiently fill the imaginations of men; and any thing beyond, besides that it leads into absurdities, has no influence on the affections or sentiments. (Hume 1779, 198)

This is a clear Hobbesian move, strongly reminiscent of Hobbes's claims that "there is no idea, or conception of any thing we call *infinite*," and that "[n]o man can [. . .] conceive [. . .] infinite power" (Section 3.1). The difference is merely that whereas Hobbes arrives at this position on account of considerations pertaining to the limitations of human imagination, Hume arrives at this position via considerations pertaining to the problem of evil; but this is not a difference in the position itself but rather in the manner in which it is arrived at.

Second, we have also seen that Hobbes maintained that despite the absence of any idea of God in our minds it is still possible to know, on the basis of a basic version of the cosmological argument, that there is an eternal cause of the world (see Section 3.1). This too is strongly reminiscent of the position that Hume's Philo ends up endorsing toward the end of the *Dialogues*:

> If the whole of Natural Theology, as some people seem to maintain, resolves itself into one simple, though somewhat ambiguous, at least undefined proposition, *That the cause or causes of order in the universe probably bear some remote analogy to human intelligence*: If this proposition be not capable of extension, variation, or more particular explication: If it affords no inference that affects human life, or can be the source of any action or forbearance: And if the analogy, imperfect as it is, can be carried no further than to the human intelligence, and cannot be transferred, with any appearance of probability, to the other qualities of the mind; if this really be the case, what can the most inquisitive, contemplative, and religious man do more than give a plain, philosophical assent to the proposition, as often as it occurs, and believe that the arguments on which it is established exceed the objections which lie against it? (Hume 1779, 261–262)

The main difference between Hobbes and Hume's Philo on this second point is that whereas Hobbes arrives at his position on account of a basic version of the cosmological argument, Philo arrives at this position via a basic version of the design argument. But the position itself, that there is a form of theism that admits of at least some minimal rational support, is shared by both thinkers.

Third, as we have also seen, Hobbes was willing to accept ascriptions of various predicates to God in an "honorific" sense, provided these predicates are not taken to stand for ideas representing the nature of God (see Section 3.1). In Dialogue II, this is precisely the position that Hume's Philo recommends as well. After having noted that we lack experience of divine attributes and having inferred from this that our ideas of God's attributes do not "correspond to his perfections," Philo goes on to say that we may still "justly ascribe" terms like "Wisdom, Thought, Design, Knowledge" to God since these terms are "honourable among men" (Hume 1779, 45).

We see then that on three decisive points, Hume's Philo lands in a position on God that strongly resembles that of Hobbes. There is some variation in the way in which Philo reasons his way to this position, but the end result seems pretty much the same in both cases.

8.2 What about Hume's Initial Lockeanism?

A problem with this Hobbesian reading of Hume, however, is that Hume endorses a Lockean approach to the idea of God in both the "Abstract" to the *Treatise* from 1740 and in the *Enquiry* from 1748, saying that the idea of God is the result of compounding ideas afforded by experience, and clearly implying that we have a positive idea of God in our minds (Section 3.5). How are we to reconcile this with the Hobbesian approach in the *Dialogues*?

One attempt at reconciliation is to suppose that Hume simply changed his mind on the question of the idea of God. A problem with this suggestion, however, is that Hume's private correspondence reveals clear Hobbesian tendencies at least as early as the 1740s, years before he published the *Enquiry*. In a letter from 1743, Hume presents the following "Objection both to Devotion and Prayer":

> [God] is not the natural Object of any Passion or Affection. He is no Object either of the Senses or Imagination, & very little of the Understanding, without which it is impossible to excite any Affection. A remote Ancestor, who has left us Estates & Honours, acquir'd with Virtue, is a great Benefactor, & yet 'tis impossible to bear him any Affection, because unknown to us; tho in general we know him to be a Man or a human Creature, which brings him vastly nearer our Comprehension than an invisible infinite Spirit. (Greig 1932, 51)

According to Russell, the view expressed in this letter coincides with Hobbes's view that we have "little or no idea of God whatsoever" (Russell 2008, 94). I believe this is correct. But how are we to reconcile this with Hume's Lockean approach to the idea of God in the *Enquiry*?

Russell's proposal is that we regard Hume's endorsement of the Lockean approach in the *Enquiry* as "less than sincere" (Russell 2008, 92, 94). This might of course have been the case. But there are at least two alternative ways of understanding what's going on here, neither of which imputes insincerity to Hume, and so might be taken to have an advantage on grounds of interpretative charity.

A first alternative is to see Hume's thought on God as undergoing a development. In his 1743 letter, we see that he was thinking about God along Hobbesian lines at an early stage, but what his position in the *Enquiry* suggests is that he might not at that point have been fully convinced and prepared to go public with these thoughts. Maybe he wanted to think this position over a bit more before officially abandoning the Lockean approach that was so widely held in his day. Maybe his thinking on this topic ripened only in connection with his work on the *Dialogues*, which might be the reason why we do not find a public defense of the Hobbesian position until this book. Neither of these possibilities implies insincerity in Hume, only caution.

A second alternative is to see Hume as engaged in a protracted philosophical investigation spanning several works, starting with a sort of hypothetical acceptance, in the *Enquiry*, of a Lockean account of the idea of God, which subsequently, as his investigations proceeded, and problems attaching to this account mounted up, culminated in the more radical position of the *Dialogues* that there is no coherent Lockean account. Toward the end of these investigations we find Hume shifting to a Hobbesian idea of an ultimate cause or intelligence behind the world.

This second alternative has the further advantage of cohering with Hume's official empiricist methodology outlined in *Enquiry* II. Assuming that meaningful terms stand for ideas that ultimately derive from sensory impressions or experiences, Hume proposes as a general strategy for determining whether a term has a real meaning, that we seek to produce the impression from which the idea that the term is alleged to stand for is derived, and if it turns out that we cannot produce any such impression this will serve to confirm our suspicion that the term does not have a real meaning (see Hume 1748, 22–25). By applying this method to the traditional Christian idea of God, it could be said that what Hume took himself to discover, throughout the course of his protracted philosophical investigations, was that it is not possible to produce the relevant impressions, contrary to what Locke had maintained, and accordingly eventually shifted to the Hobbesian view that the term "God," when used in its traditional Christian sense, is a term "without any Meaning or Idea" (Hume 1748, 28).

8.3 Was Hume a Theist?

Commentators have long speculated about whether Hume himself had any belief in God (see Kraal and Russell 2021, §10). In his works, he occasionally professes such belief. The following profession in the introduction to *The Natural History of Religion* is particularly conspicuous:

> The whole frame of nature bespeaks an intelligent author; and no rational enquirer can, after serious reflection, suspend his belief a moment with regard to the primary principles of genuine Theism and Religion. (Hume 1757, 1)

Similar, explicit professions can be found in quite a few passages (for a list of such professions, see Gaskin 1988, 219–220). Furthermore, and as we saw earlier, Hume's Philo speaks favorably in the *Dialogues* of giving "a plain, philosophical assent" to the proposition that there is some intelligent cause behind the universe (Section 8.1). There are also anecdotes from Hume's life that suggest theistic belief: the most famous being when Hume at a dinner at the residence of the French atheist Baron d'Holbach in the 1760s remarked that he "did not believe in atheists," adding that "he had never seen any" (Mossner 1980, 483).

There has been much discussion in the literature as to whether these sorts of professions are sincere. An example of a commentator who takes these professions at face value is Gaskin (1988), and an example of one who does not is Russell (2008).

By taking Hume's professions at face value, Gaskin is led to conclude that Hume was in fact a theist, albeit an "attenuated" one (similar to what I call a "Hobbesian" theist):

> my contention is that Hume gives some sort of genuine assent to the proposition that there is a god. This assent . . . is fostered by the feeling of design and given a weak rational basis by recognition that the order to be found in nature could (not must) be explained as the work of an ordering agent. (Gaskin 1988, 221)

Russell rejects this suggestion, on two grounds. First, because we see Hume concluding toward the end of *The Natural History of Religion* that "the whole is a riddle, an enigma, an inexplicable mystery" (Russell 2008, 283; see Hume 1757, 116), which certainly does not indicate any theistic belief on the part of Hume, but rather some form of agnosticism. And second, because the Hobbesian position on God that Hume ends up with was regarded as more or less indistinguishable from atheism even in Hume's own day:

> even if Hume did give "genuine assent" to a view of this kind (which I have argued he did not), the position taken is almost indistinguishable from Hobbes's skeptical view – a view Hume's contemporaries regarded as *paradigmatic atheism*. (Russell 2008, 386)

An example from Hume's day of Hobbesian theism being regarded as a form of atheism is found in Dialogue V, where Hume has Cleanthes push back against the view of Philo and Demea that theistic predicates do not correspond to the nature of God by saying that if they do not then we end up with a position no different from that of "Sceptics and Atheists" (Hume 1779, 86).

Gaskin and Russell both make good points. The evidence seems to go in both directions. The view defended in this study, that the end result of Hume's thought is that some form of Hobbesian theism is the only philosophically viable form of theism, is consistent with both approaches. The present proposal does not imply that Hume himself had any personal belief in God, not even in a Hobbesian sense, but neither does it imply that he did not have any such belief. What is maintained here is rather that the only form of theism that Hume ends up presenting in his writings as having at least some minimal rational support, as well as coherent meaning, is some form of Hobbesian theism. Whether Hume himself actually believed in any such theism, might well lie beyond what any scholarship is capable of establishing.

References

Bailey, A., & O'Brien, D. 2014. *Hume's Critique of Religion: "Sick Men's Dreams."* Dordrecht: Springer.

Beauchamp, T., ed. 2000. *David Hume: An Enquiry Concerning Human Understanding.* Oxford: Clarendon Press.

Beauchamp, T., ed. 2009. *David Hume: An Enquiry Concerning the Principles of Morals.* Oxford: Oxford University Press.

Berman, D. 1983. "Enlightenment and Counter-Enlightenment in Irish Philosophy." *Archiv für Geschichte der Philosophie* 65, 148–165.

Boston, T. 1841. *Human Nature in Its Fourfold State.* Edinburgh: Oliver & Boyd.

Bourget, D., & Chalmers, D. 2014. "What Do Philosophers Believe?" *Philosophical Studies* 170, 465–500.

Boyle, R. 1772. *Works*, vol. 5. London: J. and F. Rivington.

Burleigh, J. H. S. 1960. *A Church History of Scotland.* London: Oxford University Press.

Burns, R. M. 1981. *The Great Debate on Miracles: From Joseph Glanvill to David Hume.* London: Associated University Press.

Campbell, George. 1762. *A Dissertation on Miracles.* London: A. Kincaid & J. Bell.

Clarke, S. 1705. *A Demonstration of the Being and Attributes of God.* London: Will. Botham.

Clarke, S. 1706. *A Discourse Concerning the Unchangeable Obligations of Natural Religion, and the Truth and Certainty of the Christian Revelations.* London: Will. Botham.

Condren, C. 2000. *Thomas Hobbes.* New York: Twayne Publishers.

Descartes, R. 1984. *The Philosophical Writings of Descartes*, vol. 2. Eds. Cottingham, J., Stoofhoff, R., & Murdoch, D. Cambridge: Cambridge University Press.

Descartes, R. 1985. *The Philosophical Writings of Descartes*, vol. 1. Eds. Cottingham, J., Stoofhoff, R., & Murdoch, D. Cambridge: Cambridge University Press.

Davies, B. 2006. *The Reality of God and the Problem of Evil.* London: Continuum.

Earman, D. 2000. *Hume's Abject Failure: The Argument against Miracles.* Oxford: Oxford University Press.

Flew, A. 1961. *Hume's Philosophy of Belief.* London: Routledge.

Fogelin, R. 1985. *Hume's Skepticism in the Treatise of Human Nature*. London: Routledge.

Fogelin, R. 2005. *A Defense of Hume on Miracles*. Princeton: Princeton University Press.

Foster, S. 1997. *Melancholy Duty: The Hume-Gibbon Attack on Christianity*. Dordrecht: Springer.

Gaskin, J. C. A. 1988. *Hume's Philosophy of Religion*. London: Macmillian.

Gaskin, J. C. A. 2009. "Hume on Religion." In *The Cambridge Companion to Hume*. Edited by Norton, D., & Taylor, J., 480–513. New York: Cambridge University Press.

Graham, H. G. 1901. *The Social Life of Scotland in the Eighteenth Century*. London: Adam & Charles Black.

Greig, J. Y. T., ed. 1932. *The Letters of David Hume*, 2 vols. Oxford: Clarendon Press.

Hendel, Charles. 1963. *Studies in the Philosophy of David Hume*. New York: Bobbs Merrill.

Hobbes, T. 1998. *Leviathan*. Edited by Gaskin, J. C. A. New York: Oxford University Press.

Hume, D. 1739. *A Treatise of Human Nature*. London: John Noon.

Hume, D. 1740. *An Abstract of a Book Lately Published Entitled* A Treatise of Human Nature. London: C. Borbet.

Hume, D. 1748. *Philosophical Essays Concerning Human Understanding*. London: A. Millar.

Hume, D. 1751. *Enquiry Concerning the Principles of Morals*. London: A. Millar.

Hume, D. 1757. *Four Dissertations*. London: A. Millar.

Hume, D. 1967. *A Letter from a Gentleman to His Friend in Edinburgh*. Edited by Mossner, E. C., & Price, J. V. Edinburgh: Edinburgh University Press.

Hume, D. 1779. *Dialogues Concerning Natural Religion*. London.

Johnson, D. 1999. *Hume, Holism, and Miracles*. Ithaca: Cornell University Press.

Larmer, R. A. 2014. *The Legitimacy of Miracle*. Plymouth: Lexington Books.

Lewis, C. S. 1947. *Miracles: A Preliminary Study*. London: Centenary Press.

Martinich, A. P. 2005. *Hobbes*. New York: Routledge.

Hurlbutt, R. 1965. *Hume, Newton, and the Design Argument*. Lincoln, NB: University of Nebraska Press.

Jeffner, A. 1966. *Butler and Hume on Religion*. Stockholm: Diakonistyrelsen.

Kemp Smith, N., ed. 1935. *Hume's Dialogues Concerning Natural Religion*. Oxford: Clarendon Press.

Kemp Smith, N., ed. 1947. *Hume's Dialogues Concerning Natural Religion*. Edinburgh: Thomas Nelson.

Kemp Smith, N. 2005. *The Philosophy of David Hume*. Basingstoke: Palgrave Macmillan.

King, W. 1709. *Divine Predestination and Foreknowledge*. London: J. Baker.

Klibansky, R., & Mossner, E., eds. 1954. *New Letters of David Hume*. Oxford: Clarendon Press.

Kraal, A. 2013a. "Philo's Argument from Evil in Hume's *Dialogues* X: A Semantic Interpretation." *Sophia* 52, 573–592.

Kraal, A. 2013b. "Anglicanism, Scottish Presbyterianism, and the Irreligious Aim of Hume's Treatise." *Hume Studies* 39, 169–196.

Kraal, A., & Russell, P. 2021. "Hume on Religion." *The Stanford Encyclopedia of Philosophy* (Winter 2021 Ed.). Edited by Zalta, E. https://plato.stanford .edu/archives/win2021/entries/hume-religion/.

Leith, J., ed. 1973. *Creeds of the Churches*. Richmond, Virginia: John Knox Press.

Locke, J. 1706. *An Essay Concerning Human Understanding*. London: Awnsham and John Churchill.

Locke, J. 1743. *A Short Discourse on Miracles*. London: Robert Foulis.

McPherson, T. 1972. *The Argument from Design*. London: Palgrave Macmillan.

Mossner, E. 1948. "Hume's Early Memoranda, 1729–1740: The Complete Text." *Journal of the History of Ideas* 9, 492–518.

Mossner, E. 1980. *The Life of David Hume*. Oxford: Clarendon Press.

Mossner, E., & Ross, I., eds. 1977. *The Correspondence of Adam Smith*. New York: Clarendon Press.

Noxon, J. 1976. "Hume's Concern with Religion." *The Southwestern Journal of Philosophy* 7, 59–82.

Pike, N. 1963. "Hume on Evil." *The Philosophical Review* 72, 180–197.

Rowe, W. 1975. *The Cosmological Argument*. Princeton: Princeton University Press.

Russell, P. 2008. *The Riddle of Hume's Treatise: Skepticism, Naturalism, and Irreligion*. Oxford: Oxford University Press.

Russell, P. 2021. *Recasting Hume and Early Modern Philosophy*. Oxford: Oxford University Press.

Ryken, P. 1995. *Thomas Boston as Preacher of the Fourfold State*. Exeter: Paternoster Press.

Schaff, P., ed. 1877. *The Creeds of Christendom*, vol. 3. New York: Harper & Brothers.

Scott, G., & Pottle, F., eds. 1931. *Private Papers of James Boswell*, vol. 12, 227–232. London: Oxford University Press.

Sher, R. 1985. *Church and University in the Scottish Enlightenment: The Moderate Literati of Edinburgh*. Princeton: Princeton University Press.

Sher, R. 1990. "Professors of Virtue: The Social History of the Edinburgh Moral Philosophy Chair in the Eighteenth Century." In *Studies in the Philosophy of the Scottish Enlightenment*. Edited by Stewart, M. A., 87–126. Oxford: Clarendon Press.

Stewart, M. A. 1985. "Hume and the 'Metaphysical Argument A Priori'." In *Philosophy, Its History, and Historiography*. Edited by Holland, A. J., 243–270. Dordrecht: Springer.

Stewart, M. A. 1995. *The Kirk and the Infidel*. Lancaster: Lancaster University Publications.

Swinburne, R. 1963. "The Argument from Design." *Philosophy* 43, 199–212.

Swinburne, R. 1991. *The Existence of God*. Oxford: Clarendon Press.

Tweyman, S., ed. 1996. *Hume on Miracles*. Bristol: Thoemmes Press.

Yandell, K. 1990. *Hume's Inexplicable Mystery: His Views on Religion*. Philadelphia: Temple University Press.

Cambridge Elements ≡

The Problems of God

Series Editor
Michael L. Peterson
Asbury Theological Seminary

Michael Peterson is Professor of Philosophy at Asbury Theological Seminary. He is the author of *God and Evil* (Routledge); *Monotheism, Suffering, and Evil* (Cambridge University Press); *With All Your Mind* (University of Notre Dame Press); *C. S. Lewis and the Christian Worldview* (Oxford University Press); *Evil and the Christian God* (Baker Book House); and *Philosophy of Education: Issues and Options* (Intervarsity Press). He is coauthor of *Reason and Religious Belief* (Oxford University Press); *Science, Evolution, and Religion: A Debate about Atheism and Theism* (Oxford University Press); and *Biology, Religion, and Philosophy* (Cambridge University Press). He is editor of *The Problem of Evil: Selected Readings* (University of Notre Dame Press). He is coeditor of *Philosophy of Religion: Selected Readings* (Oxford University Press) and *Contemporary Debates in Philosophy of Religion* (Wiley-Blackwell). He served as General Editor of the Blackwell monograph series Exploring Philosophy of Religion and is founding Managing Editor of the journal *Faith and Philosophy*.

About the Series
This series explores problems related to God, such as the human quest for God or gods, contemplation of God, and critique and rejection of God. Concise, authoritative volumes in this series will reflect the methods of a variety of disciplines, including philosophy of religion, theology, religious studies, and sociology.

Cambridge Elements ≡

The Problems of God

Elements in the Series

Divine Guidance: Moral Attraction in Action
Paul K. Moser

God, Salvation, and the Problem of Spacetime
Emily Qureshi-Hurst

Orthodoxy and Heresy
Steven Nemes

God and Political Theory
Tyler Dalton McNabb

Evolution and Christianity
Michael Ruse

Evil and Theodicy
Laura W. Ekstrom

The Problem of God in David Hume
Anders Kraal

A full series listing is available at: www.cambridge.org/EPOG.

Printed in the United States
by Baker & Taylor Publisher Services